Rooted in Love:

A 40-day practice of growing self-compassion in your life and planting seeds of compassion in the world

by Lee Ann Hilbrich

Dedicated to all those who have been lights of love to me,
and especially to my helpers

Rooted in Love

I lead participants through a mini-retreat called Self-Compassion Saturday every year. This was the first big event I facilitated when I founded my holistic, creative business, Daring Discoveries. It has become a tradition to do it every year because I think self-compassion is the foundation to lasting change and growth. I would not be who or where I am without having my roots in self-compassion. I used to have the most critical, perfectionistic voice ruling me. I made a mistake and would berate myself, cursing and falling apart. Self-criticism is a shallow unhelpful root, while self-compassion is deep and truly nourishing and all about long term greatness. It took a long time to develop my self-compassionate voice, and many wise teachers to guide me, and I now have a deep healthy root of compassion in my life. But like anything, it continues to need attention and care to stay strong and healthy, and one Self-Compassion Saturday a year is not going to do that. This book is to encourage us on a daily practice of compassion.

I have found one of the best ways to create lasting change and build self-trust is to commit to practicing for a sustained number of days. The truth is, we are always practicing, even if it is just practicing watching TV daily. I have experimented with lots of different length practices over the years and I love how committing to show up every day for a dedicated time provides a container to really support and build into our lives the things our soul is yearning for us to become. It is also great for helping you exit perfectionism because at some point you will be tired and won't want to practice, so you will finally just show up imperfectly as you are and do what you can with what you have. And remember, if you miss a day or two, a B is much better than the back and forth rollercoaster between A++ and F. Practice works best when, instead of expending energy on trying to get rid of roots you don't like, you put your focus daily on feeding the roots you want to grow. If you have ever tried to practice meditation, you know the monkey mind, that mind that goes everywhere but focusing on your breath, that mind that tries to tell you meditation is pointless and that you will never be successful. But if you've continued to practice meditation, you have also learned that the point isn't to get rid of the monkey mind, and that people who have been meditating their whole lives still have it, but the point is to gently and with compassion, keep bringing your awareness back to your meditation. To me, our critical voice is like our monkey mind, it is always there, but the key is to catch yourself quickly and bring yourself back to your compassionate voice. I hope you will experience this over our 40 days together: a building up of your awareness of when you are drifting back to that critical voice, and that instead of being mad at yourself or feeling like you have failed, that you will remember your practice and with compassion and great patience, keep returning back to your foundation of love.

Each day you will receive a reflection of love. These reflections are simply stories I have caught and woven together from my life, stories that I need to remember, and I hope that they will whisper to your heart as well. You will also get suggested tangible ways to practice cultivating seeds of love in your life and in the world each day. There are so many ways of knowing things, and creative action engages the wisdom of all parts of our beings. I ask that you would remember to be kind to yourself with each invitation. Maybe reading the daily reflection is all you can or want to do, or maybe you do some activities and not others, or perhaps it is simply a spark to find your own creative way to put them into practice. I hope, no matter how it looks, you will remember to tangibly apply love to yourself daily and also, that when you are being kind to others, you will find ways to do it that feel like love and respect to yourself as well. All you really need to do is make a little bit of space each day and trust yourself, as this is not another to do list. This book is a daily dose of love, and she will work her medicine, you need only to receive and be just as you are.

"The secret is, don't discover yourself, don't transform yourself and don't recreate yourself. *Nurture yourself and see what you become.*"

-Siri Atma S. Khalsa, M.D.

There are photos to go along with each day you can find on Facebook or Instagram @DaringDiscoveries, or at www.daringdiscoveries.com/rootedinlove

If you are interested in sharing with everyone, we would love to root you on so be sure to use #rootedinlovebook so we can witness your experience.

1

Love is tattooed on our hearts

I am a fan of visible reminders of meaningful mantras and messages. When I took Brené Brown's The Gifts of Imperfection E-Course, she had us write the words, "I'm imperfect and I'm enough," on our hands and take a selfie. I still remember that moment, I remember how I was about to take my picture and I thought, wait a minute, I look horrible, I need to fix my hair and put on real clothes (I live in pajamas). At that moment, I looked down at my hand and the wisdom that I had just inked there, and I realized that this was the whole point. Even if I didn't fully believe the words I had just written there, they encouraged me, and I took that photo just as I was, taking my first step towards trusting it was okay to be imperfect and that I was enough.

I believe love is written permanently on our hearts, but since fear and life and false beliefs have often persuaded us otherwise, we need a lot of outward reminders to help us re-discover the truth. I loved the Self-Compassion Saturday year where we took it a step above sharpies and applied temporary tattoos with messages about self-love. Since the perfectionistic part of me still likes to give myself a hard time with decision making, to reduce stress I closed my eyes and picked out my tattoo message at random. It said, "All supports me and I am loved." Reading those words took me right back to how I had felt almost five years previously when I applied that very first mantra, "I'm imperfect and I'm enough," because I doubted, just like then, the message I was about to, temporarily, apply to my skin. I have a hard time always believing that the messy, pain, and challenge in my life is supporting me. I often question why something happened or wonder why I was allowed to make a decision that led somewhere that seemed to me, the exact opposite of support and love.

It was because it felt like that first message that I knew it was just what I needed to lean into and trust that year. So even though my critical voice was telling me otherwise, as the new mantra was literally adhering to my skin, I took a step and held hope in my heart that as my journey with compassion grew, I too could come to believe a new message that love was underneath EVERYthing, even when I couldn't see it. A part of our journey with compassion is to allow her messages, especially the ones we can't possibly believe could be true, to seep through our fearful thoughts and soak into our hearts that have always held messages of love.

Nurturing compassion in yourself and in the world

What are the messages you need to believe? Write or tattoo (I will leave the choice of real or fake up to you) a love message somewhere on your body that you can see as a visible reminder. Trust that over time it will sink in more than skin deep. Of course, you can always put your message up on your mirror or somewhere you will see often if you need to or prefer. I believe in you!

Write your or a message on a small piece of paper (or several) and give it out today. You don't even have to say anything as you hand it to someone you know or to a stranger or leave it somewhere to be found. Trust that love will leap off the paper and make an impression.

2

Love is messy

Oh how I hate messy, in fact, I loathe it entirely to steal a line from Jim Carrey's version of *The Grinch*. A part of it is definitely control, and a part of it is just wiring as when things are cluttered it is way too much for my sensitive sensory system and I get overwhelmed. And yet, just like the Grinch, I have also had to make room in my heart, for messy. I wish there was another way, I really do, but life is just incredibly messy and as Brené Brown says in her book Rising Strong, "The middle is messy, but it's also where the magic happens." Oh double hate on that. I wish I could say her words have sunk in deep like other love mantras I once couldn't believe, but it still makes me grimace, because while I want the magic, I wish I could just stop the mess from coming at all.

Something changed the day I read in Kristin Neff and Christopher Germer's *Mindful Self-Compassion Workbook*, "When we struggle, we give ourselves compassion not to feel better, but because we feel bad." Oh... my... goodness... My heart didn't grow three sizes that day, but I did have a moment of revelation. I have been told so many times not to judge or label or attach expectations to my meditation practice in any way, just to show up and to make space for meditation. And although I viewed self-compassion as a continual practice of coming back to the compassionate voice, I also definitely had an outcome in mind when I practiced, I desperately wanted relief from the messiness of life and I wanted to feel better! What I learned that day was compassion doesn't take away the mess, the sick, the pain, the struggle, the heartache, the grief, the loneliness, or the fear. Compassion joins us in the mess so that we are not all alone. We are our own friends when things are hard, we don't abandon ourselves in the mess, we stay with ourselves and our feelings, and we apply love. And sometimes it helps, and sometimes it doesn't seem to change a darn thing, but we keep courageously showing up for ourselves, and we keep practicing.

I have realized if I want to keep creating magic in this world I am going to have to become a lot more comfortable with messy, but I know now that I can't do that well without my friend self-compassion. And just as a friend can't make it better, self-compassion can't either, but she can be with me, filling my space with kindness in addition to all the other crap and clutter (signs of magic supposedly). I am sure I will catch myself many times still wanting her to be a fix or a maid or a magic fairy to just take it all away, but my hope is that I will practice returning to her as an empathetic friend. Sometimes compassion might make us feel better, and sometimes we might feel just as out of control, but we will always know we won't be alone in the mess. And at least, if only for a minute, if we focus on and surrender to love and what is, we won't be making things messier by adding more of our own judgments, criticisms, doubts and despairs.

Nurturing compassion in yourself and in the world

Music is also an empathetic friend to me. I love making playlists for different needs and have a "Rooted in Love" playlist you can access by searching my name, once you make a free account on Spotify. It can be fun to be open to serendipity by hitting shuffle and allowing a few songs to play and see what messages they hold for you today. I hope the songs are a resource to you throughout this journey and beyond, and maybe even inspire you to create your own love list.

Send a favorite song of yours to a friend today and let them know you were thinking about them or just share it online. It might just help someone to hold onto hope in the mess today and take courage. You could even get really crazy and call someone up and sing them the chorus of Stevie Wonder's song, "I Just Called to Say I Love You."

3

Love guidelights

Do you have those people in your life who encourage you to love yourself and see the best in yourself, even when you can't or don't know how yet? Kristin Neff, Brené Brown, my husband, my psychologist, my acupuncturist, my yoga teachers, colleagues, friends, family, and more have led me in the way of love. Honestly, I am still not sure how acupuncture really works, but I know that getting poured over with kind words from my loving acupuncturist and having a forced 20-minute nap while the needles are in definitely works! We have to be able to see and imagine another way before we can begin to travel down it. When someone provides you with genuine kindness and comfort that you wouldn't even begin to know how to give yourself, you begin to believe it is possible to go down a new path. And, when you've been doubting your own path for a while, and they look like they are doing alright, almost maybe even happy, you tell yourself that maybe it is worth a shot.

That friend who checks in on you at work, and listens to you with kind eyes, leads you to reflect and wonder if you could also notice yourself with the same warmth and gentleness. That coach or counselor who helps you see that perhaps you really are doing the best you can, encourages you that maybe you can stop being so hard on yourself and trust yourself a bit more. That spouse or family member or friend who, when things go wrong, doesn't freak out, but instead holds up hope and makes the best of what is, makes you believe that maybe you can start to respond with compassion instead of reacting with fear.

Even though we are each walking down our own paths and can only see a small portion illuminated ahead and the rest is in darkness, when we look up and out we can always see other lights shining in the distance around us. We may not be able to see how to get from where we are to there, and it may be tempting to stay where we are even when we know it is not working or safe, but we have to trust that we have all the light we need to keep taking the next steps towards those warm glows. I know you may not believe it now, I definitely didn't when I first started walking this path, but trust me that one day, you too, will be radiant house of light and love others can spot and be guided by from the dark and critical space they are in.

Nurturing compassion in yourself and in the world

Light a candle today or have a fire. Just spend a minute gazing into the flame and release anything you want to be deconstructed and allow the light to open your heart to new possible ways of traveling lighter and more brightly in this world. Maybe you can catch a sunrise or sunset too!

If you can, spend time today with someone in your life who models love for you. Allow yourself to be shaped in the presence of their love and thank them for being a guidelight for you. Or, you can just pick a person, someone you actually know or anybody in the world, dead or alive, who is an example of love to you, and allow their spirit to guide you through the day in how you imagine they would love themselves and others well.

4

Love is a sea turtle nest parent

Sea turtles are so brave to me. They are left alone to hatch and find their way to the sea, often led by the light of the moon, or nowadays, runways and nest parents and spectators. When I first heard the term "nest parent," I thought it was a turtle, but as learned, they are actually human volunteers. On busy beaches where sea turtle nests can remain because there is no driving allowed and because there are organizations looking out for them, the nest parent will mark the nest with the assumed date of egg laying and the anticipated due date, and keep watch over it and protective boundaries around it. When the nest is getting close to hatching, the nest parent puts up runways that help guide the babies safely from the nest down to the ocean (think of the kiddie bumper rails in bowling that keep the balls out of the gutter).

I find our critical voice often tries to get us to believe that runways or bumper rails are for babies or kids, and that when we grow up we put childish things like them and compassion behind us. Usually there is resistance to self-compassion because it feels like we are babying ourselves and that to really make it we have to be hard on ourselves. Life is hard enough on its own and yet so rarely do we give ourselves permission to live with more ease and kindness. The truth is, self-compassion truly does have your best interests at heart. She doesn't care if you have polluted yourself with critical words or disparaging and severe remarks, she is there for you, willing to help protect you, even from yourself, and is cheering you on when you take a step in being gentle and loving with yourself. Even if, and especially when, you feel like an awkward turtle.

We cheer for sea turtles because they are so little and vulnerable, and yet, they are doing it! Awkwardly and bravely they make their way to start their new lives. We too look like that, even when we put on our grown-up masks. The truth is, if we are brave with our lives (and you are if you are reading this book), then we are going to keep dreaming new dreams, and trying and birthing new things in our lives, no matter how old we get. We are going to be vulnerable and look awkward and be beginners, over and over again. We may have seasons or points in our lives when we find ourselves not pulling out self-compassion as often because we are living it, but we can't forget that we are never too old for runways or cheerleaders, and that we absolutely have to be as kind to ourselves as nest parents when we are first starting out on a new way of being.

Nurturing compassion in yourself and in the world

Take a minute to think or preferably write down what permission you need to give yourself as you are just beginning this journey. So often adults don't do new things because they are scared not to be good at something and perfectionism can give us a hard time when we are being brave. How can you be your own cheerleader and boundary protector during this season of vulnerable change and growth within? Trust the process and know that mistakes are a valuable part of it.

Try loving in one way that feels new or different or perhaps just requires you to be a bit brave today. Remember to put up the runway and rails, that it will most likely feel awkward, and that you have already been brave in so many ways since you took your first journey into this world.

5

Love takes breaks

I am a sucker for research. It has helped me meditate daily, play and rest well, and of course, practice self-compassion. The research from Kristin Neff, one of the world's leading experts on self-compassion, or as I like to refer to her lovingly in my mind, the Self-Compassion Queen, shows that compassion gets us further than critical ever will, and it is true. Critical might work for a while, but it doesn't lead to lasting change, and it has a great cost to it, we are literally attacking ourselves, leading to chronic stress and survival mode.

I know a bit too much about living in stress. I also know, theoretically, that I am meant to be kind and rest on the journey of life, but I am the worst at putting this wisdom into action. I keep buying into the myth that there will be an end to the to-do list, or that I can squeeze in just one more thing AND THEN, I will finally take a break and rest. And yet, I keep learning that life is one messy complicated construction project, full of disappointments and setbacks, and times of complete deconstruction and overhauling. I would never make it in the construction business, patience for days those souls. I was in awe when we hired a contractor to finish out a barn for my art studio and I would watch as he and his small crew of one or two, took many frequent breaks, sitting in chairs outside and snacking on pecans. They weren't on their phones, they weren't doing anything but enjoying the day and each other's company. They were my role models during that project. And even though I hated waiting and how slowly it seemed to go, every time I saw them taking a break it inspired me that I too, should probably be taking a real break (which meant not on my phone and preferably outside) even when the things I was working on were not done and everything was beyond messy. Instead of just pushing through, criticizing myself the whole way, and ending up stressed and exhausted, I was being reminded there was always a compassionate choice. I could instead stop my judgements and unrealistic expectations of myself and life, and accept it all as part of being human. I could simply take a break.

I love that Kristin Neff has made a very practical template for practicing self-compassion that she so wisely calls, The Self-Compassion Break. It is only 3 phrases, so it is really easy to remember and each phrase is based on what research has shown are the three components of self-compassion. My favorite part is the common humanity element because it provides this recovering perfectionist with the data that suffering happens as a part of life and not because we weren't perfect enough. We all need self-compassion on our life journeys of deconstructing and constructing, and preferably before we get to the point of utter exhaustion and burnout. The Self-Compassion Break is a great foundation and it is best applied frequently throughout the day and it goes like this:

This is a moment of suffering (mindfulness)
Suffering is a part of life (common humanity)
May I be kind to myself (self-kindness)

Nurturing compassion in yourself and in the world

Put the self-compassion break out where you will see it often and apply it at least once today. You could get creative with decorating or displaying it, and/or you could tailor it by making up your own phrases using wording that works best for you. Hopefully it will be memorized soon! You could also give yourself a real break today!

Make a kind gesture for someone else today. Offer a shoulder rub or hug, draw them a bath, share a piece of dark chocolate, or make them a cup of tea. You don't have to tell them you are giving them a self-compassion break, but just shower them with love and let them experience how good it feels themselves to take a moment of rest in compassion.

6

Love moves forward mindfully

I didn't know how to be kind to myself or treat myself like a precious person. All I knew how to do was beat myself up when I was already feeling bad, crazy, or when I made a mistake. When things were messy, I was a mess too (and not the mindful element of self-compassion where you recognize stress without getting swept up in it). When I felt out of control, I started becoming controlling. When something went wrong, I helped make it worse. For example, the time I drove too quickly into the garage and ripped off my side-view mirror. I made it even worse by throwing a fit and cursing myself and all my days. I know, but at the time it felt like the end of the world. All I could focus on was how I had failed and cost us money and time in the future to fix a problem I had unmindfully created. All I knew was the critical voice.

I had to learn the compassionate voice and how to move forward with love when life didn't go the way I expected or wanted or I was (gasp) human. It was other people showing me what it could be like, and then it was continual practice to catch the patterned ways of responding and, instead find ways to love myself well with words and actions. We all have little losses and deaths throughout each and every day and if we pretend they don't hurt or respond solely with more hurt, we are only burying the pain temporarily. When we allow them to surface and be seen and comforted with love, they can truly heal and be transformed. Now, instead of berating and blaming when I make a mistake or experience a loss, or at least as quickly as possible afterwards, I try to tell myself that I did the best I could and that I can make the best of whatever it is now. I also allow myself a good cry if needed because grief is real, even if it is only over a side-view mirror.

In addition to practicing in the moment, I have also returned to the past, because sometimes, as I have learned from Brené Brown, to move forward mindfully, we need to go backwards. When we begin to see and process our current suffering in new ways, it can be so helpful to return to previous difficulties or seasons where we were so hard on ourselves, or maybe where we just never even acknowledged the amount of stress or suffering that was occurring. It can also be little moments or interactions not so far off that stick with you. I am often not my best when caught off guard and yet I can ruminate and beat myself up that I didn't respond a certain way. Why did I give in so quickly to a stranger's needs over my own, why didn't I say something to stand up for myself and others, why haven't I figured this all out yet, and/or why do I keep shrinking instead of standing up? It really does change things in the present to go back and see our situations with compassion and speak or write kind words over them and that person, who even then, really was doing the best they could.

Nurturing compassion in yourself and in the world

At the end of the day, do a review in your mind and see if you missed any moments of suffering where you could have applied compassion. You could also go further back, if you wanted, and apply compassion to a minor past difficulty or stressful season where you were unkind to yourself. It works really well to journal through either using the three components of Kristin Neff's Self-Compassion Break, doing what she calls Self-Compassion Journaling. It is never too late to view yourself through a compassionate lens and to remember you have always been doing the best you could!

If you find yourself waiting at all today, try taking that time to practice a moment of mindfulness. Maybe at a stop light you take some deep breaths instead of checking that text. In line at the store, or while waiting for your gas to pump, you could notice those around you and send them love in whatever way works for you. If you walk anywhere, you could use that time to really be aware of your surroundings and take them in deeply. You can inspire and help to create a more mindful caring world today!

7

Love doesn't edit

My faith community has done a good job of normalizing for me that it is okay to share our stories - we all have the good, the bad, and the ugly. It was hearing other people be brave and authentic and share their stories that included light and dark that helped me realize no one is perfect or has it all together (the common humanity element of self-compassion). I know and wholeheartedly believe in this and almost always practice it in-person, and yet, there is something about online space that seems to make it almost too easy to just leave out the ugly pieces. I am drawn to the people on social media, or in any type of media, who tell it how it is. I breathe a little sigh of relief that I am not the only crazy one. And yet when I go to share my posts, I don't even mean to, but I often catch myself only sharing a part of something or the half-truth. To be honest, when I choose to share on social media it is usually because it is a good moment, but then if I never share the bad moments, pretty quickly it can be heading towards a picture-perfect feed.

When I remember, again and again, I recover and start reminding people that I am human too and add in the unedited soundbites and the rest of the pieces of truth for a more complete picture. Love doesn't edit because it knows those might just be the pieces we need to connect to each other. For example, just because I am posting how excited I am about my upcoming event, because I really am, you should also know that I have moments where I am dreading that I agreed to do this because I am so tired. I also have nights where I wake up, anxious and breathing shallowly, thinking about all I have left to do or figure out. So there. It is really not that hard, but that lull to picture perfect can sneak up on me before I know it.

Love doesn't edit because the truth is love knows there is space for every single part of us. Love knows our hearts are big enough to hold all the pieces, and that each piece is precious because it is a piece of us and makes up the whole masterpiece. Love doesn't have to cut things out or crop or enhance, because love knows there is nothing we could do to separate ourselves from the love that we truly are. Love can see the big picture and it is begging us not to throw away pieces we think don't fit. Just like us, love gets pissed when it has worked SO LONG on a puzzle and at the end there are missing pieces. I can't tell you how many times I have thought something was a mistake or a waste of time, or just not worth keeping, only to discover later on how love had a plan for that piece and how it might serve myself and others way before I could see it. Often, the best thing we can give pieces like that is lots of unedited space and love.

Nurturing compassion in yourself and in the world

If you are anything like me and turn to social media when you are feeling stressed, take the time today to curate your social media feeds, filling them with voices of hope and truth that make you feel not alone and enough just as you are.

Post some ugly online today. Share how it really is sometimes, because we already know about how it is good sometimes. Help someone else to breathe a bit easier knowing they are not the only one. Or maybe you just share that you are on a journey of self-compassion with someone.

8

Love your own voice

"Oh darling." I can still remember Kristin Neff's words and tone like it was yesterday. I was in a conference ballroom getting some continuing education hours for my counseling license and she was the speaker. I had no clue what I was getting myself into and how much this leading researcher of self-compassion would plant seeds at that time that would change my life. All I knew was that everything in me rebelled when she spoke those two words, "Oh darling."

She was giving an example from her own life of a time when she was applying the self-kindness component of self-compassion and that was how she started off talking to herself, "Oh darling." I hate to admit it, but I felt a little bit sick. It might have been disgust, and I was definitely thinking, "This is absurd, I would never talk to myself like that." I mocked her tone in my mind and I almost dismissed her message because I just could not ever see myself getting to that point. I felt like a hopeless case. And honestly, if that is what it took to be self-compassionate, I wasn't sure I wanted it.

Poor Kristin Neff, she doesn't know it, but I now use her as an example all the time when I am educating on self-compassion (and I think I do a pretty perfect imitation if I may say so). But I share the example of her voice and words now, not because I am judging or scared of it, but because I want people to know that when you are learning about self-compassion from others, you should never expect to end up with their words and their voice. We need others to show us the way, to show us what is possible, but we must each realize that our own compassionate voice will never be exactly like anybody else's voice. You are on a journey to find and develop your own voice. And for a while, that may mean trying on others' voices and phrases, just like you try on clothes. Who knows, I haven't said an "Oh Darling" yet, but there may come a season when it fits.

Nurturing compassion in yourself and in the world

Self-compassion includes learning to love our own voice and sticking with ourselves through the awkward times when it just seems insane what we are telling ourselves. I know you have heard, you don't have to believe it for it to work, and it is still true. So just start where you can today. Focus on finding some self-talk that does work for you. Try talking to yourself with kind words or with some endearing terms, just as you would an animal or friend you love. View it as an experiment and don't rule anything out, just for today. Hopefully you will find a phrase or term of love you can live with without feeling nauseous.

Put some love and kindness out into the world today. Speak an encouraging word to someone you know who is being hard on themselves or tell that stranger they are beautiful or doing a good job. You may just give someone a word or phrase to hang onto and grow in their life. When I was first transitioning to being an entrepreneur, something I never thought I would do because perfectionism for so long told me that would be too risky, we had a couple over for dinner and the husband told me, "Dream big and believe in yourself." He probably didn't give those words a second thought but they encouraged me and I painted them on a canvas that I still display today.

9

Love online

The internet is a double-edged sword for me. While I constantly have to keep it in check and not allow it to rule me, addicting me to its dopamine hits and its ability to take me away from my present reality at any moment, it has also been a source of connection and strength. I have found compassionate voices online, people I never would have met in person, and I have allowed myself to be filled with their love. And they have no clue, but I am soaking up each kind word they speak into the world.

I still remember the morning I woke up in the guestroom bed by myself. Even though I don't remember at all what the fight/meltdown was about that culminated with me deciding to sleep alone in the other room, I do remember exactly how I felt when I woke up that morning, and it wasn't good. I felt absolutely hopeless, overwhelmed, and paralyzed. At that time, I was a new entrepreneur and had burned myself out with the exhaustion that is legally and professionally setting up a business and trying to make all of my ideas happen at the same time. I literally never stopped working and had worn out myself, and my family. So, I did what everyone does when they wake up feeling like this, I scrolled through Facebook. And somehow, thanks to the magic/creepiness of algorithms, I saw an encouraging video by a man named Brendon Burchard. I had no clue who he was, but he got me out of bed that day. His offering was simple, "When it feels like there is no hope, simplify. Wake, work toward just a few focused goals, ask for help, breathe and keep faith." It seemed he got it and had been there, though, and it was his love and belief that helped me to get out of bed that day. He gave me the compassion that I needed to learn how to give myself.

I have found other compassionate voices online too, sometimes as part of a course I paid for, and sometimes just voices who are sharing love freely through posts or videos. They have led me in the way of love by tuning my neurons to new frequencies that weren't about living in stress, fear, or survival mode. If you come across someone who strikes a chord in you, just remember, the chord is in you. We are for sounding boards for each other and the compassionate people you find are truly just reverberating back the love that is already a part of you, maybe just a bit lost. All you need to do is tune into their frequency, allow it to resonate within you, and trust that your compassionate voice is there and getting stronger each day.

Nurturing compassion in yourself and in the world

Use your voice today to make some sounds to send out into the world. Sing out loud, chant, vocalize, and don't hold back. Love hears you and is getting you back online.

Reach out and let someone know that they have been a source of love and guidance for you. Send them a note or email or direct message of gratitude, thanking them for the love they have shared and letting them know that it didn't just go off into the unknowns of the interwebs, it went directly into your heart. You could even be brave and use your voice for a heartfelt message or recording to give them, or if you are able, support their work with your finances or by sharing it.

10

Love rests and plays well

For a long time, I did not allow myself to rest or play. I believed resting or playing were unproductive, and somehow had a voice in my head that said, "We must always be productive." It took learning about the value of play and rest from Brené Brown's 10 Guideposts on Wholehearted Living for me to begin to give them a chance. Apparently, they are biological needs (which of course I am sure you knew)! I also began to learn from the researchers in those fields, such as Stuart Brown, that play and rest might not be as purposeless or unproductive as they at first seem.

When I discovered there was research by Moreau and Engeset showing that free playing with LEGO® bricks could influence creativity, I decided to test it out and committed to building creativity every day for a year by playing with LEGO® bricks. It was like my dream ticket as it gave my controlling brain the convincing it needed to let my inner child play every day, but that didn't mean it was easy, especially as it was a whole new medium for me. Resistance is real and I can only begin to tell you about the voices in my head when I started that year of building without instructions. They were screaming for their lives that I was so stupid to waste my time playing with a child's toy each day for a year, and they almost won. It was only thanks to all the courageous souls who have been creative with their lives before me that I was encouraged to go on. That year of playing well really unblocked my creative magic in so many intangible ways, and as a bonus, I did create a productive online course so others could experience the magical lessons I learned as well.

The same sort of thing helped me with rest. I had learned the hidden value of rest to help with immune issues, resiliency and more during my yoga teacher training in restorative and vinyasa yoga. So, for a period of 40 days, I chose to let go of productivity and take on resting on my back in Savasana, or corpse pose, each day. I know you may think that sounds easy, but trust me, committing to rest every day was SO hard. Turns out, surprise surprise, I had a lot of resistance to softening and surrendering. I even paid, and not a small amount, to take an online Savasana Intensive course by two restorative yoga teachers during that time, because I needed the encouragement to keep faith in the importance and value of the practice of resting. Life doesn't need to be so serious or fast paced. When we trust love, we trust there is time for play and rest and that maybe they are closer to the purpose of life than we think. And if you don't trust love just yet, or are wired anything like me, maybe just trust the research, and begin to see where it takes you.

Nurturing compassion in yourself and in the world

I sign off all my monthly e-letters, "Play AND Rest Well," because I still need the reminder to take the time for those crucial needs. What is one way you could play or rest well today? It may just be to go to bed earlier. Notice if your critical voice starts to get loud as you make a plan, and as Brené Brown suggests, write down on a post-it note what permission you need to give yourself to do it anyways. Keep your permission slip with you or somewhere visible to encourage you.

Squirrels always remind me to be playful. Be like a squirrel today and put a post-it note out in the world somewhere with a message to encourage whoever discovers it to play and rest well. You could even get creative and leave a gift with it like a tea bag or some LEGO®. By simply playing and resting well know you will inspire others who see it or with whom you share about it and help give them the permission to do the same.

11

Love is simple

I can often make things a little too intense or complicated, or maybe a better word, a little too perfect. I go out into my day thinking I need to bless every situation and it has to be big or extravagant or hard, and then I get stressed and don't want to open myself up to the world. I already struggle enough with waking up in the morning, not in an anxious state, and if I add all that pressure I will never get out of bed! The truth is we don't actually have to fix situations or even try to make things better, we only need to love and accept ourselves and others just as we are. It really is that simple. In my uncomfortableness with messy and uncertainty and suffering, I am quick to make up a story and put a label on a situation as good or bad, thinking I know the answers and what is needed. I observe everything around me and in the world and I just get overwhelmed. Or, I look at myself and my life and see all the things that I think are problematic or need to be different. Any movement I take towards change from that space of stories and expectations will not be sustainable or very helpful. Love instead reminds me to trust the wisdom of a seed, that it has everything it needs inside itself, and that my greatest offering is to simply notice and nurture what is with love.

As we know, most seeds are actually quite small, and over time, we also know the great complex systems they are capable of becoming with a little tender loving care. We can't make love grow, all we can do is provide the ample support and help to remove any obstacles. That means the simple things, each and every day. With gardening, it is things like when we notice plants are drooping and we water; when certain times of the year we shield plants from the scorching sun; or when we fertilize, weed, and simply spend time being with them. Humans aren't so different. We only need to pay attention to ourselves and others and sometimes all it takes is a real smile, a loving gesture, a genuine greeting, a warm hug, a kind word or nurturing action, and love can take root and grow in that moment, continuing to blossom in ways we might have never foreseen.

When I let go and start tuning into the love inside of me and listen, when I am open to how love wants me to move, not how my ego wants to show up or what my anxiety says I should do, I almost always discover it is such tiny, easy, simple things for others and myself. It is getting outside of my own story that day and being present with others I encounter - whether a clerk, office cleaning person, or a friend - and offering my smile, eye contact, or listening ear; it is picking up a piece of litter I see on a walk; it is writing a letter to someone on my heart; or it is stopping whatever I am doing or emoting to greet and appreciate my husband when he comes home. The same goes with loving myself, it is so often not the grand big gestures, it is truly just checking in with myself throughout the day. That can look like pausing for a moment of compassionate movement to loosen up my tight muscles; applying an essential oil to help me; getting up to get a glass of water instead of staying thirsty; releasing expectations; or letting myself go out when the sun starts shining even when there is work to be done. Love doesn't have to be complicated, it really is those small matters of attention to those around you and to yourself that add up big time over the long run.

Nurturing compassion in yourself and in the world

Be open to the simplicity of love today. Make one simple gesture of nurturing love towards yourself today and trust that it will really make a difference. Let go of thinking anything is wrong with you as change truly happens when we feel loved and cared for, just as we are.

Let go of any expectations and just gift your home or the world with a simple seed of loving awareness today and trust that it is enough. You might be amazed at how your small kind attention creates a ripple effect in someone's life or in the world.

12

Love is a knitter

My mother-in-law taught me how to knit on a really long road-trip. I suffer from car sickness, so I was hoping knitting would distract me from feeling nauseated. I never really planned to progress past a simple scarf, but over the years, since I have learned, I have made socks, stuffed animals, and more. I will never forget working on my first big project though. I had decided to knit a throw blanket. I had dedicated so much time to it and was around halfway finished. And then it happened. I discovered a hole. I had apparently made some mistakes and there was a giant hole in my blanket, and it was continuing to unravel and grow. I freaked out. Instead of calmly taking a break and thinking about who I could ask for help with this issue, I proceeded to rip out all the work I had done while sobbing that I had just wasted decades (okay maybe weeks) of my life and swearing I would NEVER knit again. I was beside myself and an absolute and utter mess.

What I wish I could have told that younger version of myself was, love is a knitter. I wanted to give up because I thought I had wasted time and my work was beyond repair, but the truth was, in every imperfect stitch I had made, I was learning something, and nothing is ever wasted. Knitting, as it turns out, is all about embracing the handmade imperfections. That gigantic hole (which in hindsight probably wasn't even that big) - someone could have helped me to unknit so I could go back and fix it (it would be years before I managed unknitting myself and it is still tricky). Or I could have used extra yarn to sew it up, or to at least stop the unraveling process. The point is, I wasn't a true knitter yet. Because knitters spend an exorbitant amount of time with their projects. They are truly laborers of love. And they don't give up. They may have to rip out or even start over if the pattern is that complex or they are that much of perfectionists (hey no judgment here), but they get back in there and use whatever they learned and they try again. Now-a-days, I rarely unknit or rip out. If I discover I have been doing a pattern wrong, oh well, I course correct and, it is still hard, but I allow it to be a beautiful imperfection.

I haven't gotten to the point yet where I deliberately add in imperfections. Author David Anderson shared the following on his "Deliberate Mistakes" blog post: "I'm told there is always an imperfection deliberately woven into the corner of the [Navajo] rug. It looks perfect—then there's this 'mistake.' Except it's intentionally put there. Why? The Navajo say it's 'where the Spirit moves in and out of the rug.' That's hard for us to understand. God's Spirit moves in and out of imperfection? a 'mistake'? We've spent our whole life trying to get rid of all

35

imperfection." I wonder, though, what it would be like if we trusted love enough to know that each stitch of our lives is never wasted, even if it feels like a huge gaping loss or mess, because love is a seasoned knitter, and she won't give up on us. And perhaps that she is even closer when there is space for her to be needed in our lives. What if we really trusted that she will either leave the imperfection in because she knows it will be cherished one day, or that she will stick with us as it feels like we are going backwards, but really things are just being unknitted so they can be knitted together in new beautiful ways.

Nurturing compassion in yourself and in the world

Take the time today to make or do something by hand or from scratch. As you slow down and work on it step by step or stitch by stitch, really pour your love into the process. Enjoy or share with others! Remember, our relationships are often complicated knitting processes. If that feels daunting, don't forget it could be as simple as a card, a meal, or even the bed. Or release a perceived past failure.

Make a small business or a creative person's day! Maybe you buy art from a friend, supplies from a non-chain store, or food or drink from the farmer's market; give a positive recommendation; become a patron on Patreon; send a note or message of appreciation; or purchase handmade online.

13

Love is one word

I tend to make things more difficult than they need to be due to my own worry and fear, and that is on a good day. Enter in a messy life season or project, and I go straight to the big picture and think about all the things that need to get done or be fixed and I freak out. I am getting better at allowing and trusting the messy layers on the canvas in my creative practice, knowing if I keep showing up magic will happen, but I find myself fighting and resisting them when they are on the canvas of my life. When I was having one of those messy times in my life, as you do if you are alive, a dear friend sent me the song "One Day" by Christa Wells. The chorus goes:

You're doing one day, one breath, one prayer
One thing at a time
One word, one step, one hope
In a coming light
Don't try to swallow the ocean
Keep doing one day
'Til one day you're free

One. I was so struck by it. I realized this song was so powerful because it was taking me back to the present moment. If we focus on this one day, this one breath, we enter the present where worries about the future or ruminations about the past don't live and therefore can't keep us stuck or curled up in fear in the fetal position (if you are anything like me). We let go of our attachments and surrender our plans and can just be in and with the present moment, trusting it is divine and all a part of the plan. We can forget since we never have to intentionally breath that we have this amazing ability with our breath to move into conscious breathing. We can take a slow deep breath, get present, and then do the next ONE thing, not all the things, from that centered connected present place.

I love a line in the bridge of this song as well, "Oh, I see you laughing on the other side." It's so hard for us to see through to what is coming next when we are currently living in the out of control mess. It is so hard to believe that one day the mess could possibly just be a layer that got us to another layer where we are LAUGHING. Even harder maybe to believe that not only could we be laughing, but we might also be at a point where we are appreciating some beauty from that mess that still shines through and got us to where we are now. When we can't see past a messy layer, we can keep coming back to our breath and the present moment. Love will see us through, one breath at a time, whether we are conscious of it or not.

Nurturing compassion in yourself and in the world

Whether it is a messy, scary, or unknown season of life, one really deep breath of love is always available to us, so breathe fully and consciously as much as you can today. Maybe you could even spend time soaking in breathing and being present by practicing a pranayama (breath control exercise). Some of my favorite breathing techniques are box breathing and alternate nostril breathing. And today, instead of focusing on all that is still messy, give yourself credit and celebrate the things you did do, even if it was only one thing.

Chris Germer has a free audio/written meditation available on his site, *chrisgermer.com,* called "Giving and Receiving Compassion." It is basically a breathing meditation where you breathe in compassion for yourself and breathe out compassion for others and is a great practice anytime of the day.

14

Love is not perfect

I remember very clearly a vulnerable moment I had while I was at the training to become certified in Brené Brown's work. I was in the small group that I had been learning with over the past few days and we were taking turns sharing our individual projects on shame and authenticity. My turn had come and gone but I was not fully present as the next couple of people were sharing, I was in my head. I realized it was staying small if I stayed there, so before the next person started sharing I spoke up courageously and spilled what was on my heart.

I told them I noticed that everyone else had received or was receiving feedback after they presented their projects, but no one had said anything after mine. I do not like to ask for what I need, I know it is hard for most everyone, but as a five on the enneagram I am all about being self-sufficient. So while it might not seem that vulnerable, for me, it was big time to take up more space and put my needs out there. And do you know what the group said to me? They told me that I had presented my project so perfectly - almost like I had wrapped it up like you would a package and put a bow on it - that they didn't think I needed any feedback. They told me they thought I had it all together. The truth was most other people were sharing current, still vulnerable stories. I had chosen my project on an old story about how I used to pretend everything was fine in the early days of my marriage when really it was deteriorating and unhealthy. Shame kept my problems hidden and it wasn't until we got to our breaking point, as is the case unfortunately for most couples, that we started telling the truth and being authentic and getting help. It was also then that I realized I had missed out on a connection with a friend who had also been struggling in her marriage, because I had been presenting as perfect. And here I was again, missing out on connection with this group of people because of my issue with perfection.

This was a pattern for me. I often sort all my hard stuff out first and then choose to share it with my friends and family after the fact, because I want to control perception and prevent any judgement, and because I definitely don't want to feel vulnerable. Learning about self-compassion has helped me to begin to let go of my perfectionism and let others in, and it is still a work in progress. It is so scary for me to let someone in when it is still messy, because when I am vulnerable, I don't know what will happen. And then, what if I say or do something that isn't pretty or perfect, what if it is awkward and I regret it later, or what if they judge or don't love the messy real me? The truth is, I have to love the messy real me first. I am learning that true love doesn't want us to be perfect, just to be ourselves. It often feels safer still to put something out there that I think will be pleasing to all than it is to do the hard work of connecting in the moment with my heart and other people. I have caught myself many of times when there has been a tragedy or injustice in the world wanting to look at how others are responding so I can be doing the right and perfect thing, instead of getting still and feeling with those who are suffering or have suffered, and moving from that heartfelt place of compassion. If we want to connect with love, however, we can't shut her out until things are better or less messy again. We have to let her in to those vulnerable, scary, dark, real places, and it is then that we are reminded and remember that there is nothing we could ever do or be that would disconnect us from who we truly are, love.

Nurturing compassion in yourself and the world

Brené Brown says to overcome perfectionism we have to explore our fears and change our self-talk. Take some time to journal and/or explore what you fear people will see when you let them in. Come up with a new mantra that helps you remember why you want to let go of perfectionism. Mine is, "The cracks connect." I used to spackle every hole in the wall or imperfection in my home, never realizing how exhausting it was always trying to keep up appearances, especially when I applied that to trying to control how I appeared to others. Now when I catch myself trying to please and perfect, or worrying about what people think or if I am enough, I try to remind myself my imperfections are lovable, normal, and connecting.

Let someone see you today when you don't have it all together and are perhaps scared or snotty. Make that phone call even when you know a feeling will pass and let a friend in on your mess. You will be gifting yourself and them with connection. Or show up even when you are having a hard time or not feeling your best and trust the offering of yourself as imperfect is actually just what is needed. It isn't just the hard things that are vulnerable to share either, so you might even tell a current, close to your heart, desire or dream or need to someone who matters to you. Or, something that is often hard for me, you might allow yourself to lead or teach in a new area that feels vulnerable and not as polished or competent as you would prefer.

15

Love without armor

Oprah says when describing letting go of perfectionism in Brené Brown's The Gifts of Imperfection E-Course, "People try to be perfect because they think it might make them more lovable. But really being perfect doesn't protect you from being judged, it protects you from being seen. And really the only way to be truly loved is to be open and to be seen for who you are - in all your glorious imperfection." I know this is the truth, and yet it is still a battle somedays to not pick back up the false armor of perfectionism. Even though I know it will actually hurt more in the long run because I will be shrinking from my authentic self and my values, it still calls to me, whispering how good it will feel to be shielded from everyone and everything. I am sure I am not alone in wanting to go back to old coping strategies, especially in times of family get-togethers.

It is actually thanks to those times though, that I have been learning to see with more compassionate eyes. I am becoming more aware and noticing quicker when the voices in my mind are yelling at me that "It is not worth putting yourself out there," and "Just be small and be perfect and then you won't offend anyone and everyone will like you." And it is then that I have the opportunity to pause, reflect, and view myself, and my family, with new compassionate eyes. It is then that I can realize how younger perfectionistic me was doing the best she could, as of course all of my family was and is. We all have triggers and get wrapped up in identities and lies, and we all make up stories, it is just our nature.

While we can't control the stories others tell, as there are no shields strong enough for that, we can control the stories we tell ourselves. I am tired of judging the journey, I don't want to judge younger me, and I don't want to judge myself or others now. Instead, I want to love myself well, reminding that scared, imperfect me that I am enough. I want to hold myself in a space of grace as I find a new way to show up, a way that is protected not with armor, but with self-compassion, permission slips, and boundaries that work for me so that there are still chances for genuine connection and love. I want to remember that as I try and fail again, there is beauty in that messy space too as I begin again and again to practice seeing more clearly with my new eyes. I don't want to lug perfectionism to every gathering and I don't want to lug old versions of myself and my family and friends. I want to greet every person from a new space that allows for us each to unfold in that present moment, in all of our "glorious imperfections."

Nurturing compassion in yourself and in the world

Make a list of 10 things you love about yourself. Read it often and definitely remember to have it in your back pocket in situations where you feel vulnerable. Remember you are precious and you are more amazing than you think, and you are always doing the best you can, even when the armor is up. Also remember what Brené Brown says about boundaries, "Daring to set boundaries is about having the courage to love ourselves, even when we risk disappointing others."

Try living today believing that others are doing the best they can and meeting them without all your past histories. If you notice you literally can't spell histories without stories, so give yourself, your family, and everyone a gift by meeting them in the present without expectations.

16

Love says relax

I am in love with witnessing animals roll over on their backs in the grass. I was a cat person for the longest time, scared of the responsibility of a dog, but when I watched a friend's dog just roll in the yard so full of play and so empty of care, I knew I had to adopt a dog. Animals have so much to teach us if we will only slow down and be with them. Dogs aren't the only ones who enjoy rolling on their backs, I have also seen horses, pigs, and even, a rabbit thoroughly enjoying themselves in such a way. I remember how I couldn't tear my eyes away the day I saw, through my window, the wild rabbit roll over, exposing its white stomach, seeming to melt into and dance with the grass. After several minutes where time seemed to stop as I was entranced with this soft lovely moment, the rabbit finally righted himself from his playful time on his back, and hopped away, but the scene didn't leave me so quickly.

It reminded me of a picture I have of me as a young child. I too am laying on my back in the grass, and notably, I have one hand palm resting up and one hand palm resting down. I feel like that picture is my essence, and yet I so often forget about her. Her hands remind me that balance is good and necessary – that it is right to ground down and take care of me and that it is also right to be open and giving up to the world. She tells me it doesn't have to be either or and she tells me that it doesn't have to be so hard. It really can be easy, I can relax and just be me because all supports me and I am loved. If you are anything like me you probably have a lot of resistance to relaxing and softening, and yet, love has our backs.

Those animals that seem extra on guard – like deer and bunnies – show us what it is like to live brave – because we do see them. They come out and do their animal things – grazing, playing, etc. – showing up even though there could be danger at any moment. They don't let all the scary and terrible things in the world keep them from living lives full of simple pleasures. Seeing that rabbit be so stretched out and exposed, I thought about how I don't trust that I can stop running and doing and protecting, how instead I keep my walls up and my armor on. If vulnerable animals can do it, we too can stop rushing and racing around, and truly rest, even if for the briefest of moments, in the soft grasses of love.

Nurturing compassion in yourself and in the world

Let down your guard today and allow yourself to unfold and relax into a moment that feels exquisite. Maybe that means laying in the grass, taking a nice bath, oil self-massaging, curling up with a good book, just being still, or releasing some heavy armor into the Earth. It is essential to take care of yourself and treat yourself as good as you would a precious animal companion. Dogs are so direct with their needs, they know what they want and they aren't afraid to ask for it persistently or jump into your lap to get it. Be like them today - don't hold back and be super clear – even if that means a growl.

Animals teach us about the ways of love without any words at all as they speak to our hearts. Show them some kindness today. Maybe it is just spending extra time loving on your pets, or perhaps it is rescuing an animal from a shelter, or supporting a sanctuary or wildlife organization with time or money. It could be making the environment for wild animals more loving by planting things they like in your yard or by picking up any trash you see outside. If you use or eat animal products it might be buying from organizations or farmers that care about animal welfare standards and therefore reducing support for factory farming.

17

Love is a blessing

I never really appreciated or understood blessings until I had a transformative awakening experience to them. Before then, I knew about blessings of course - bless the food, receive a benediction, and the "bless you" after a sneeze. And I knew I felt rubbed the wrong way by the "I'm blessed" catch phrase and all it implied. But what I didn't know is what it felt like to be intentionally held and blessed in a such a sweet way that I couldn't help but come into a whole new relationship of appreciation and discovery with them.

It happened when I attended my first ever art and yoga class. I went because I had heard the message from several people that I should go to Village Art and Yoga and since I loved yoga and creativity it just seemed right. To my surprise it wasn't the type of vinyasa yoga I was familiar with though, it was art and Kundalini yoga. I had never done Kundalini yoga before and thought it was totally weird (I still do sometimes, but it is also totally awesome). That aside, the part of the class that touched me the deepest, was the blessing sung at the end. In that tradition, as taught by Yogi Bhajan, they use an Irish blessing called "The Long Time Sun". The blessing was sung to us by the teacher and we were also encouraged to sing the blessing for ourselves and to sing it for someone who needed it. It goes: "May the long time sun shine upon you, all love surround you. And the pure light within you guide your way on." It could have just been due to the genuine love of the teacher, but it was such an intentional and powerful blessing experience for me. In addition to feeling like a hug for my soul, it sparked new thoughts and questions in my mind... "I can bless myself and others?" It felt so strange, but also so right.

I started incorporating blessings into my life after that experience. For example, I read and received blessings from John O'Donohue's book *To Bless the Space Between Us* and then wrote out specific ones to send in letters and cards. After learning they could be helpful and healing for my autoimmune thyroid condition, I used essential oils to bless myself and then began to share the blessings of essential oils with others by making special blends for them and for my events. I blessed my food and my water after hearing about how doing so can literally change the structure of both as they respond to us and our words. I began to recognize more when I was being blessed and tried to allow myself to receive it and also began writing them down in a blessing journal. I made my own blessings and incorporated them in my courses and here is a blessing I want to give to you today:

May you feel the warm light of the sun on your skin and know
that a light just as powerful and pure also shines within you.
May you hear the wind blow through the trees and trust that
your spirit too is full of praise and the ability to move through
all things with ease.
May you open your eyes to see wonder and beauty today and
allow it to open and touch your heart and remind you how
deeply you are cherished and loved.

Nurturing compassion in yourself and in the world

What blesses you and touches your soul? Try incorporating one self-blessing into your life today or asking for a blessing. It may be new or different, but blessing yourself has got to be better than beating yourself up so give it a try.

Be on the lookout for one way you could be a blessing today. Remember it doesn't have to be anything big, and sometimes your greatest blessing might be right at home, but be open to your power to bless and help transform our world with more love. I love this prayer by Grace Alvarez Sesma: "Creator, bless my eyes that I may see love, bless my lips that I may speak love, bless my ears that I may listen to love, bless my heart that I may give and receive love, bless my hands that all that I touch feels love, bless my feet that my walk may be a prayer upon Mother Earth."

18

Love is greatly blessed for a tuesday

There was a season where every Tuesday I would travel to a satellite office at a Church in downtown Houston to see psychotherapy clients. There was an elderly man who volunteered on that day to staff the front desk at the Church. I would arrive and we would greet each other, and every time I asked how he was, he would smile and tell me, "Greatly blessed for a Tuesday." When I realized that was always going to be his response, I became annoyed as it seemed inauthentic. As time passed, however, I began to look forward to our ritual interaction. I mean, I could have stopped asking how he was, I already knew what the answer was going to be. And yet it was comforting in a way to hear his choice to focus on his blessings, as I am sure he must have had all the things that come with aging such as health concerns, losing friends, etc. It made me question how I have come to view that question. At first, I felt like he was denying his feelings and being unwilling to share his story, and then I realized that is his story. No matter what is going on in his life he is controlling what he is focusing on, and his heart is focused on all the blessings he has on a simple Tuesday.

His simple consistent answer made me wonder about how I respond to life each day. I don't think it is healthy not to share the hard things on our hearts or to think we can never say something sucks because someone else always has it worse, but I realized that I had gotten into a complaining habit and always seemed to allow a "Not Enough" to creep into my answer. "Things are going so well, but I'm so tired," or, "My schedule is really the way I want it, I just wish my health was better." My perfectionism was keeping me from ever being fully satisfied with anything. My lens so easily shifts to lack, fear, and all that is undone and ugly in my life and in the world. I wondered if instead I could just allow myself to be Greatly Blessed, if only for one day a week. I know that I came to enjoy him telling me how he was because he was reminding me of a truth I often dismissed. No matter all the little things - all the ways I try and control my life, my health, my work or my relationships; all the ways I choose to label things as good or bad; all the expectations and "shoulds" I hold - I am greatly blessed. It was only my thinking that made it otherwise.

That is what gratitude and love does, it brings us back from us being the center of the universe, and reminds us that our perception may be off. I mean really, who are we to truly know what is actually good or bad for us? I am tired of labeling some things or some moments as beautiful and others as not. I want to be thankful and see beauty in each moment, because I know when I am thankful and making that choice, I am bringing love to it, and that really is going to make it all beauty full. We spent all of two minutes conversing on a Tuesday once a week, but he was a messenger of love to me, one I resisted at first. He reminded me not to take for granted all the little and not so little things I often did, and he reminded me it was my choice to separate things out as blessings and not blessings, instead of believing and receiving all of life as a blessing.

Nurturing compassion in yourself and in the world

I need more than a weekly reminder to choose to see beauty and have found my best seasons have been ones where I was practicing my blessings or gratitude tangibly every day. If you don't have a tangible way you practice gratitude yet, maybe start today. Commit to receiving whatever comes your way today as blessing and respond by writing or speaking gratitude.

Spread some beauty perspective today by pointing out and/or sharing the beauty and blessings you see in the world. Call someone's attention to the clouds, a rainbow, or a moment of serendipity that happened.

19

Love goes before you

With this 40 day practice we are all focusing on the same purpose of deepening our root of love, but I also lead an online course called 100 Days of Building Creativity, where I invite people to build anything they want into their life and provide support, encouragement, and resources. For 100 Days of Building Creativity 2018, I was practicing how I tagged it on Instagram: #100daysoflovewithspirit. The following unattributed quote I found on someone's Instagram feed and promptly put on my phone lock screen during the project sums it up: "Each morning I consciously choose to be blessed and be a blessing in this world." My plan was to bless others in secret with love (and obviously not post and share about that) and to practice daily compassion and love for myself. I had no clue how it was going to look each day as that was the point, to let Spirit guide me (which led me unexpectedly to begin writing this book about love).

On day five, I got quite the surprise. I was scheduled to teach yoga that morning and I was out of fuel in my body, in my pantry, and in my car. Everything was running on empty. Instead of forgetting to fill up and then getting into my car without having travel time allotted to get gas, like I usually do and then proceed to speed and swear, I actually remembered my lack of fuel in advance. Since the gourmet coffee beans were out and tea wasn't going to cut it with my lack of sleep, I decided to grab a caffeinated drink from a well-known coffee establishment near the gas filling station before heading to the studio, something I rarely do. In being kind to myself with my situation that morning, I also realized I could do something else I hadn't done in a long time, pay for the person's drink in the line behind me. I was so excited. You can imagine my surprise when I pulled up to pay for my drink and for the car behind me, and was told by the cashier that the person in front of me had paid for my drink. Wait what?! I was going to do that! And how does that even happen? "I consciously choose to be blessed and be a blessing in the world."

Love goes before us. Literally in this case too as I had let that love car go before me when we both approached the drive-through from different directions. We already have it all inside of us, sometimes it is not until we give it away though that we see it was always with us, leading the way before us and coming back behind to us. Truly we are surrounded by love and may we keep paving the path of love in our lives so that others coming after us will never be able to forget it either. Choosing the path of love may seem like a small act, but know that it builds and each day we will see and experience more magic in our lives.

Nurturing compassion in yourself and in the world

Let's keep building on blessings. Be open to opportunities to receive love today – from yourself, from others, and from the world. That may mean making some buffer space so you have room in your schedule to move with love. This is something I still work on but what a difference it makes when I do have margin built into my day – I am less reactive and more loving and open. I am hoping you too will be surprised at how loving yourself and others well truly creates a circle without beginning or end.

Pave someone's way with love today. Buy their meal or drink or leave them a gift card at a store and show them that love is always before them. Or at home show a family member, room-mate, or neighbor that you were thinking of them by going out of your way to set up something appreciative or special. No matter how small you think it might be, those little acts matter.

20

Love leaves notes

I love discovering messages. I used to take photographs while I was running, inspired by the character Allison in the movie *Yes Man* (immediately watch if you haven't seen it a gazillion times like me). I would even store my compact camera in the holster around my hip designed for a water bottle. Having my camera with me on runs made me notice more and it set up a tone of looking for beauty everywhere that has continued for me long past my running streak.

Whenever I am outside now, usually walking my dog, I am alert for what words, messages, and signs I might find. Or sometimes I am just going through the motions and rushing my dog while listening to a podcast or completely in my mind. But on the good days, I am looking for love notes. And I have found my fair share. Some I know were intentionally not for me, like the sidewalk chalk messages that it looked like a friend set up for someone's run/race: "You're doing Great," "Hey I Love You," "And You're Hot," and "Almost Done," but I took them to heart anyways. And some I wonder if they just got left behind or dropped, like the uncolored mandala sheet or handwritten note.

A lot for me are just part of the natural world like a feather or an acorn or a wild animal sighting that might mean more to me than to someone else. And then there are those that are truly intentionally left, like a painted rock with encouraging words. I know they are all pretty simple things but discovering items and moments when I am on just an ordinary outing really make a big difference in my day. They become more than what they are, they become truly love notes from the universe, helping me to believe a bit more in myself and in this world.

Another fun place to discover messages – your mailbox! I love writing and sending notes because nowadays most of our mailboxes are not places of love and long notes from friends, they are bills and junk mail and catalogues. Has getting a handwritten note ever made your day? Have you ever kept a letter or message you received, holding onto words that touched you? Even in our digital age, there is still something special about sending cards to each other. Even when we have social media to keep us up-to-date throughout the year and we can print a picture so cheaply now at home, we still like to send Christmas cards and photos and we cherish the ones we get. I think it is fun to write letters all year round, sending people words, images, or gifts I find that make me think of them. My hope is that discovering those surprises in their mailboxes helps them to know love is always trying to get in touch and passing notes.

Nurturing compassion in yourself and in the world

Take your camera or your journal out with you today and be alert for messages. Perhaps you even take the time to write yourself a message, documenting in a letter about where you are on this journey of unconditionally loving and all you are hoping it will bring you.

Leave a message of compassion out for someone to find today. It could be as simple as a post-it note a family member or co-worker will find or you might paint it on a rock or canvas and leave it somewhere for a stranger to discover, or perhaps you really write out and mail a letter of love.

21

Love listens

When I first learned about the benefits of meditation from my psychologist and felt called to start meditating, I was terrified. I was so worried that when I got still and quiet I would hear something I did not want to. I know now that I was projecting my critical voice and my fearful self. Because at that time, all I knew was how to be hard on myself and I was always feeling like I should be doing more or that I wasn't measuring up. Instead of my anxious reality being confirmed, I found compassion when I finally let go and listened. Meditation has become such a sweet space where I can just be. Sure, it is still hard and my monkey mind is all over the place a lot of the time, but it is truly a space where I listen to and connect with myself and my divine. And my fears have never once come true in four years. I rarely hear anything in meditation other than sound of my own breath (and my dog whining for me to be done). There have been a couple of times I did receive a new direction or unexpected idea, but it was never anything at all like what my anxiety dreaded.

I think it is only natural that we put what we know onto other people or the unknown. We make up stories based on what we know, and when you only know fear and the critical voice, that can be problematic. There was the day, years before I started meditating, that I was going to walk away from my Church. I felt half-hearted and like I couldn't measure up and that, if I wasn't all in, I needed to leave, because I was sure that was how God felt too. Of course, the day that was to be my final time, we weren't having a typical sermon, we were being led through a listening practice called Lectodivina. You can do it with any sacred text, listening to a passage being read aloud slowly three times, with pauses in-between to see what you hear. It was the forced silence and space that I needed, but wanted to run so far away from. And do you know what I heard, I heard the word "surrender." And I started crying. Because it wasn't a yelling, mean, forceful surrender, it was a let go, relax, you are loved, stop trying so hard, surrender. All of the sudden it was lighter and easier, I wasn't alone, and I was cared for, loved, and wanted, just as I was. It was that day that I felt God was love, and I could hold on to that.

It can feel really vulnerable to open yourself up to listening, especially to yourself. That is why I love creative practices. Because I am often resistant to pausing for times of reflection, processing, and gasp feeling, getting creative – whether that is free-playing with LEGO® or clay, coloring a mandala, free-association journaling, art journaling, or moving natural materials around on a walk – gets me out of my head and things come up that I unfortunately might not have welcomed or noticed any other way. Literally, at my workshops on my sign-in sheets it informs, "The creative process could bring up unpleasant feelings or thoughts." But thank goodness it does because when we can see and hear ourselves in new tangible ways it really can open us up to being able to understand and thus care for and love ourselves even more.

Nurturing compassion in yourself and in the world

Truly everything is speaking to us if we can only pause and listen. There are so many ways to meditate and listen so make space for listening to love and yourself today in whatever creative way inspires you.

Really give the gift of listening to someone else today. If someone shares something with you, no matter the format, don't jump to your own story or the next topic, really reflect on what they put out in the world and offer back to them what you heard, saw, or felt. It will truly be a gift.

22

Love is aware

Learning how to listen to myself and process my emotions with love was huge. It truly is amazing how when the critical voice is strong we can judge ourselves so harshly just for being human. Brené Brown says in *Dare to Lead*, "Without self-awareness and the ability to manage our emotions, we often unknowingly lead from hurt, not heart." Hearts require quiet listening, and often whisper about subtle healing shifts. Hearts desire for us to become sensitive and attentive to our needs, truly alive, and in love with ourselves and with the world. Learning more about our hearts, how we are wired, and what we value is definitely a way to increase compassion with ourselves and have empathy and generosity with others.

Learning "Input" was one of my Gallup strengths helped me be more compassionate with the piles of papers I accrued and all the resources I kept, and over time I learned to trust myself more, keep less for myself, and share more with others. Learning I was a "Highly Sensitive Person," as described by Dr. Elaine Aron, and from other sources that we all have sensory thresholds helped me to stop labeling myself as bossy or controlling, and realize instead that I was just trying to manage my environment so I could function without withdrawing.

Learning I was an "Observer" on the Enneagram gave me permission to finally start acting on the urges and desires I had for more freedom and space without feeling guilty that I wasn't a good friend or leader. When you find ways of seeing yourself that allow you to have more empathy and love for yourself, you often also realize just how hard you have been on yourself for simply having unique intricacies, sensitivities, and wirings, and it can be life-changing. When we know and love ourselves fully, we are sharing that more instead of judgment, shame, hurt, or misunderstanding.

Even if you don't know why you are acting how you are, or you don't know why your body is doing what it is doing, you can always listen with love over fear or hate. For example, I have struggled for a long time with my diagnosis of Hashimoto's, an autoimmune thyroid condition. I have received so much contradicting information that many times I am simply paralyzed trying to make sense of what all is really happening and what is actually helpful to do or not. I have definitely given up at times. Finding Stacey Robinson's book, *You're Not Crazy & You're Not Alone*, was such a gift. I still don't know a lot of things and I still deal with Hashimoto's, but I am aware that the most healing thing I have ever done is decide to love and trust myself and my body no matter what. I am now thankful for the awareness that diagnosis and my other autoimmune health conditions have given me. They have made me listen and go down avenues of healing and growth I might have otherwise never discovered. They have made me get really clear on what is most important to me and what I am willing to spend the energy I do have on. They have made me have more compassion with myself and others. In fact, I am not sure I even want to be restored anymore, but I am very open and excited about the possibility of transformation and healing in ways that are beyond what I could have even imagined for myself. We always have a choice and we never want to allow something other than love to tell us who we are. We can choose to be curious like a good therapist or coach would, and lean into whatever is there, nurturing and trusting what is, allowing it to guide us to become more aware and awake in whatever way it may be asking. We can always do this for others too, holding them in love, even when they don't know what they are feeling or what they are doing.

Nurturing compassion in yourself and in the world

Spend some time connecting with your heart today. Maybe even place one or both hands over your heart and just listen for any messages of love she wants to give to you.

Don't strive or try to make anything happen today. Trust your energy and urges if you have any and follow your heart. Know you have invisible support and guidance always with you.

23

Love is a shapeshifter

There was a time in my life that I thought I should only be one size, for the rest of my life. That thought has long since passed, but it still tries to take root every now and again. I used to tell myself, if you keep the boxes of bigger clothes, then you will just be allowing yourself to get back out of shape. What I have come to discover, however, is that love is a shapeshifter. It doesn't care what shape you are or what size you are, all it cares about is how you feel and how you are treating yourself. I have been way underweight and still thought I wasn't thin enough, so I know love is an inside job.

I now am the proud owner of four treasure boxes on the top shelf of my closet, each marked with a different size range. When I most recently transitioned to a bigger box and put away some smaller clothes for another day, instead of feeling devastated, I was actually quite excited to get back to some sweet items that I used to love wearing. I was so thankful then for the compassionate me who had lovingly stored them instead of getting rid of them. But that tendency to think that I should be in a smaller box and that I am doing something wrong by being in the box I actually am still creeps in. I catch myself making comments like "I am too big," or "I have got to get in better shape before _____," fill in the blank. Or, I start thinking that I am going to get out of control and run out of boxes. Those are not helpful things to say or think, and they lead nowhere but to boxes of desperation and unsustainable change. So, I try to come back. I remind myself that there is no one way to be, that there are so many factors with my health and environmental conditions, and that even if I end up having to buy more clothes and boxes, the most important thing is that I am loving and accepting myself exactly as I am. The most important thing is also that I am trusting my body and participating in her deep healing, not just changing her outward appearance to the detriment of my health.

Loving myself still means I ask questions and get curious and make changes, but, with love, it comes from a place of trust and acceptance instead of fear and disgust, and that makes a world of difference. Self-compassion always wants us to be our healthiest best selves, but she reminds me that won't happen from a shallow root of criticism that will have no lasting standing or true nourishing base. I don't want to hustle, be extreme, or allow outside factors to dictate how I think I should be anymore, and I am tired of my focus being on trying to get to a shape or stay a shape. Now, if I am concerned, I would rather be looking at why I am reverting to old patterns of stress response, or how I could reduce my toxin load and increase my nutrients and energy, or just plain have compassion for the strains of the season and trust my body is doing the best that it can and love it, no matter what shape it shifts into.

Nurturing compassion in yourself and in the world

Do you have clothes in your closet that are too tight or too loose? Make yourself some boxes or update your boxes so that all your clothes feel just right. You deserve to feel comfortable right now, and punishing yourself with too tight or not buying yourself the right size in fear that your changes won't stick and you'll just be wasting money is not how things will truly shift. If this invitation doesn't fit you, try applying radical acceptance to any area you wish was different in your life - mental or emotional state, family, fertility, health. Fully embrace the shape that area currently is and allow love to fill it.

Thinking and talking nice about my body is still something I have to watch and work on, in front of myself, and others. It is really hard, but also really powerful to make a list of 10 things you do appreciate about your body. Even if you can't honestly say you love your body's shape, commit to expressing appreciation for what you can. That act will be a radical example of body love for our world.

24

Love doesn't break tofu presses

Not many people have gotten to see this side of me, but I used to have a problem with throwing more than just a fit. I would throw anything - words, punches, furniture, remotes were a favorite - and most recently, even though it had been so long I couldn't remember when the last time I had a throwing episode was, I threw a tofu-press. When I threw the tofu-press it was a wake-up call. I did not want to go back to where I had been at one point in my life. Usually I would throw something in a burst of anger and once I realized what I had done, I would keep going because I was so ashamed and figured I was already a horrible person and ruining everything, so I might as well blow it all up. I used to not know how to cope with or express my emotions or fears in a way that could be heard. I couldn't tolerate disappointment, imperfection, or misunderstandings, so I just acted out and made things worse because I was hurting. I created the disconnection I was experiencing and fearing with my angry actions, and I hurt objects, and unfortunately for a time, the people closest to me too.

I felt so disappointed in myself when I threw that tofu-press, which was right after I had slammed the freezer door repeatedly, in case you were interested. I felt like a failure because I hadn't broken something in so long and yet I had circled back there again. I curled myself into a ball in a chair in my art room and cried. I wouldn't let my husband in because I felt so small, and because I wasn't sure the anger had passed and I really didn't want to go back to hurting more than just objects. It may not seem like it, but that was a healthy response for me. I was in a safe spot and I was allowing myself to feel my feelings. I eventually allowed my husband in and I processed my shame with empathy from him. I also processed the experience with compassion for myself by exploring my needs and stressors and what had happened to make me susceptible to falling back into old habit energy. I also apologized, because even though it has taken me way too many years and it can still be a challenge, love definitely apologizes.

And I found out something unexpected, I was told I hadn't broken the tofu press. I don't know how I didn't as I had definitely chunked it across the room, but it was still okay. To me that was such a beautiful gift and metaphor. We don't always truly know what the state of things are, and often when we think we've gone backwards and we act like it is all over, then it really is. Instead, if we can apply compassion with whatever bad situation occurred, there is the possibility of the healing power of love, and seeing that maybe things aren't the same broken mess after all.

Nurturing compassion in yourself and in the world

How do you treat yourself when you fall back into non-serving habits and patterns or when you feel unlovable? "Shoulding" on or being hard on ourselves, avoiding, or ruminating is not the way of compassion. Make a loving plan. It doesn't just have to be big things either. Every day we are human we will probably reflect on the day and realize there were things we did that we are not proud of. The important thing is to be able to bring them into the light of awareness as soon as possible so we can forgive and grow, instead of hide from or bury them, and that takes love.

Utilizing Brené Brown's research on shame and vulnerability, tell someone that you want to be in their empathy seat when they are curled in a ball of shame or ask someone to be there for you. Discuss what that means to each of you and how you can be there for one another when one of you needs to be reminded of the healing power of love and connection (There is a great animated RSA short video made to go along with Brené's explanation of empathy vs. sympathy and that could be a nice place to start and is available on her website at *brenebrown.com*). You could also decide to be a well of empathy today and bring that healing energy everywhere you go.

25

Love yourself

Yoga for me, for a long time, was just another physical fitness avenue. I never expected to become a yoga teacher and I still won't forget when someone new visited the studio I had trained at and asked me which of the type of classes offered burned the most calories. I had deep compassion because I knew exactly what it was like to only exercise if it was going to "burn calories." I could only hope that yoga would lead her on a loving journey as it had with me. When I discovered my first yoga teacher, yoga changed from just exercise and it started to become more about play, fun and growth, and loving myself. Then I found an additional teacher and it started to also become about restoring, quieting my mind, and meditating. Then I found another teacher and it started to also become about nurturing my soul, connecting to my divine, and freeing myself. I am so thankful for my many beautiful teachers. I now know that the practice has always been my teacher and that it hasn't changed, but as I change it continues to be a mirror and reflect back to me what I am needing on my journey.

Yoga was the gateway into learning to take time for myself every day and to discovering a subtler level to myself and my experiences. I initially began practicing asana, or the physical postures of yoga (which is actually only one small piece of what yoga is), for very outward reasons. But as I kept showing up to my mat, I found so much more within and realized that yoga, and perhaps myself too, was deeper than I could have ever imagined. Yoga is sneaky like that. It has helped me in so many ways to cultivate self-compassion for my body, mind, and soul because it transformed into a time I carved out of the day for myself, not to just exercise, but to listen to and love myself. It is now a little ritual of self-love because I have had teachers, in-person and online, who have encouraged me to be kind to myself as I practice, to apply self-massage, to breathe, and to know that re-wiring the mind takes time and it will all come.

When I am practicing asana at home I don't always set it up beautifully like how it is for you in a studio. Some days I literally roll out of bed in my pajamas and right onto the soft rug there on the floor next to me and find some movements that feel good. Other days I have more energy and roll out my mat and maybe I diffuse an essential oil or light a candle. But now instead of trying to "work out," I am trying to tune into my body and what it might be needing that day. Some days it does want to work hard, but other days or seasons it needs a rest. And I am FINALLY trying to listen and honor and respect my body's needs and seasons, trusting even though it is so hard, that if I rest now I won't just stay resting forever, that I will want to play and work hard again.

Nurturing compassion in yourself and in the world

Whether yoga is your thing or not, check in with yourself today in whatever movement way works for you and give yourself the love you are needing. Sometimes instead of pushing through and doing what the plan was, we just need to be heard and honored, breathe deeply, shake it out, give ourselves a hug, dance, rest in child's pose, or simply be. Love yourself well today.

Invite someone to practice yoga, or whatever pathway that connects you to your body in a loving way, with you and let's start a love yourself revolution! If you are interested in trying yoga, I definitely recommend you check out a local studio first. If only online is available to you, I now use and love the app Glo because I love so many types of yoga, but my first online teacher was Yoga with Adrienne. She generously provides free yoga for all and has several practices suited to self-compassion, so search Yoga with Adrienne on YouTube with any of these titles: "I Love," "Self Love Yoga," "True Self Love," or "Love Yo' Self."

26

Love meets you where you are

I never ever thought that restorative yoga would one day be my favorite type of yoga. My exact thought might have been, "Why on earth would I take an hour to just rest, that's crazy, no one has time for that." I can still remember that young me at the gym who ended up in a yoga class where there was a really long Savasana at the end of class and I couldn't lay still and felt panicky and like I was going crazy. It can take a while to get to loving to restore, but now, I wish we could do Savasana the whole class and absolutely love restorative classes where you rest in supported poses, meditating and relaxing. One of my favorite parts of restorative yoga, if you have never tried a class, is all the props. Literally there are cushy bolsters, blankets galore, sleep masks, and the most essential prop – cozy socks, the cuter the better. There are so many lovely props because restorative yoga is all about supporting your body so that it can fully relax, surrender, and restore, and you can't do that if you are in pain or uncomfortable. The props help to literally bring the earth up to meet you where you are, basically saying that there is nowhere to go or to get, that you are absolutely divine exactly as you are. How compassionate is that?!

I wonder what it would be like if we all allowed ourselves to use props in our actual life, giving ourselves the support we need each and every day. Because, as much as we try to deny it, being creatures of achievement, progress, and stability, each day is different, and that includes changes in our bodies, our minds, our energy, and our circumstances. Yet so often we treat each day the same and we expect at least the same things of ourselves, and most of the time more than the day before. Then, when we don't measure up, we beat ourselves up or assume something is wrong or we are going backwards. And we rarely, if ever, appreciate and think the differences are beneficial. For example, I had several days where I was so tired and I couldn't figure it out as all the usual culprits couldn't be blamed. I went with it and slept more and did less even though it still bothered me, and then I realized with a tell-tale sign in my throat that my body had most likely been trying to fight off a cold that my husband recently had. Once I realized that was it, I was even kinder to myself and was so thankful my body had slowed me down and was expending its energy on keeping off illness instead. It makes me sad though that my first line of thought is often not to thank or trust my body and its wisdom, but to judge myself.

What if, instead of making judgments, we make adjustments. Consider if we choose to give ourselves grace each day, appreciating and accepting and supporting just where we are and what we need in every new day. We choose not to view giving ourselves what we need, even if we didn't need it the day before, as failing or not enough, instead, we view it as loving ourselves well. Can you imagine if we all lived by that restorative manifesto? Love meets us where we are and it knows the truth: Life is not about how far we can stretch in a yoga pose or how much we can achieve in the world, life is about loving ourselves through it all.

Nurturing compassion in yourself and in the world

How can you support yourself today? What do you need to put in place so you can be more relaxed and at ease with what is, and is maybe even beneficial, instead of struggling and striving? Now gift yourself with some life props. Also, if you want to try a restorative pose at home you could simply do legs up the wall pose. Grab those comfy socks then scooch near to a wall and swing your legs up and lay back. No need for the hamstrings to be super straight and you can be further from the wall if they are tight, just allow the blood to flow the opposite way for a while and enjoy. This also works great with laying on the ground and with your legs bent resting them up on a couch, chair or bed. And it may just be me, but I love legs up the tree.

If you see someone struggling today, be a human prop. Hold that door, take that picture, carry that box, or offer a cool or warm drink.

27

Love does less

Sometimes when it comes to loving ourselves we think more is the answer. I was attending an Art and Yoga Teacher Training by Hari Kirin Khalsa and Krupa Jhaveri, and while we were being led through yoga one morning, I felt something release in my body, almost like when you have water in your ear and you finally get it out, like something had been unblocked. I remember going up to the teacher afterwards and telling her my experience. I told her the movement we were doing when it happened and said something to the effect of, "So that means I should do more of that right?" She had just been calmly listening to me and then she simply said, "Not necessarily." Well okay then. It got me thinking, how often do I jump to the conclusion that because something was helpful to me once or worked out well, I should do more of it?

I fell into that trap with running. Running started out as such a good thing for me, I truly loved it and what it did for my mind and body, how it opened my heart and lungs, and what it taught me about the power of practicing. I loved how it got me outside and it was so fun to discover a whole new world (seriously it is

81

a whole other world). But I allowed goals and achievements and fear to dictate my journey instead of listening to my body and my adrenals. And so, six years after I did my first couch to 5K, my body stopped loving running. Literally, the thing that used to recharge me, now depleted my health because I had done too much of a good thing and wasn't running sustainably or in a way that was listening to love. Sadly, it was listening to my fear of losing running or losing my gains that actually led to just such a result. It can also be hard for me to discern that not everything is forever and I am often guilty of just adding on to my daily personal practices without taking things away first, oblivious to the fact that if something works, eventually it should also decompose and be done at some point. In my health journey, I won't just make one change at a time to see how it goes, I will implement all the things I have read could be good for me at one time and try and speed up my healing. Because of course more doesn't come by itself, it has also been packaged together with quick and fast results.

We have to keep learning that it is okay to let go and that sometimes it is going to look like less, but that is not necessarily bad. I loved the day I was trying so hard to transform in a new season of life with many practices and I came across the poet Nayyirah Waheed's words, "let a new life happen to you." I stopped almost all of my agendas that day, much to my ego perfectionist self's horror of losing a winning streak, and allowed myself to wait and see what love had in store for me to pick up that season. Now that was a challenging practice. However, when you apply love, you will always get enough because it is love that actually heals us. Love is always with us and giving us just what we need, and we don't have to try to store it up or keep trying to find it or make it happen as quick as possible, we just need to be available to receive. And that means having hands and lives that aren't full of more.

Nurturing compassion in yourself and in the world

Instead of asking what more should I be doing, maybe try asking if you are still being kind to yourself? What can you let go of or do less of today? What is something that maybe worked for you in the past but is no longer what you really need? This could be a habit or practice, plans, relationships, or maybe literally stuff. Allow love to show you the way and sustain you instead. And don't forget going forward, as Anne Lamott wisely reminds us, "'No,' is a complete sentence."

Help our world have less junk in it so we can notice more of love. Maybe try one of these: Pick up litter you see, take the time to recycle, donate rather than throw away, choose to use non-disposable items, or start a compost pile.

28

Love naps

Essential oils work great, if you actually have the energy to get up and get them. But then there are those days when the walk to the kitchen where you store your magical oils seems just too far. Sure, you can just see them from the couch in living room, but they might as well be a million miles away. And so after you've eaten the healthy Nutella (Justin's chocolate hazelnut butter) straight from the package; scrolled online too many times to count (even though every time you see something in the world that is unsettling you say you'll stop); sent numerous texts to your person (and to send anymore while they are working and you are wallowing would just feel wrong); finished your library book (that made you laugh and cry and feel like you need to stop everything and have champagne and celebrate the preciousness of life tonight); you do the only thing you can do, you crawl off the couch onto your most favorite softest rug in the world, lay face down, and take a nap. You don't even have the strength to turn the light off that is right next to you.

Does anyone else have these days? Well if you are out there, at least you know you have got one "me too" right here. And it doesn't really matter the reason I don't think. We each have our own varied and unique reasons and they are constantly in flux.

Mine usually consist of the moon, my monthly female cycle, my autoimmune health issues, and my physical and emotional sensitivity to all things, but sometimes I just get too tired to even try and make sense of it all. I just need to surrender to the nap, no matter the reason.

I have a mental battle I have to fight the entire way – telling me about all the shoulds – the newsletters that aren't going to write themselves, the toilets not scrubbed, the dishes that literally all you need to do it put them in the dishwasher, and of course the "who do you think you are," with all the people who don't get to take naps in the world, but finally, I give in to the rug and to the nap. I allow myself to be supported by the earth, by love, and I trust that while a nap can't fix everything, time spent on the soft rug in retreat is the most loving thing I can do for myself and the world at this moment.

Nurturing compassion in yourself and in the world

Take a nap today. If you aren't a napper (just wait), try a 20 minute Savasana on your version of the softest rug in the world. Yoga Nidra is also amazing (and yes, I know you are supposed to stay awake during it for maximum benefits, but falling asleep is often a good enough effect for me).

The next time you are having a can't get off the couch nap kind of day, tell someone. Let's bring back napping as an acceptable act of love. Maybe you'll give someone who thinks they should be doing more permission to do the same. I loved when I posted this reflection online and a sweet friend commented, "Embrace the nap so you wake up to embrace the rest of your day... or not. Maybe you'll need more nap. That's ok. It's just one day."

29

Love is our nature

I know we are all wired differently in how much we love the outdoors, and different outdoor environments are pleasing to different people, but I don't think we can deny that our bodies respond to the daily rhythms of light and darkness and to the change of the seasons. We think we can be separated from nature, but the truth is we are nature. We are made up of water and plants and air. We too are fleeting and will one day return to the earth. When we spend time connecting to the ground and getting outside of our perceived walls, we are reminded of these truths, and we see that nature can help guide us to live life well.

I used to hate weeding, it was a chore, but then I was gifted a perspective change. I began to view it as a practice where I could be outside and learn from Mother Nature and tend to my soul as well. And I discovered buried treasure – seriously! Have you ever seen what happens when some leaves decompose? They turn to gold! As the brown plant matter decays away, there is a stage where all that is left is a golden skeleton of connecting veins. It is beautiful. And I think we are like that too.

So often we fight the impermanence of life. We think because we worked so hard to get somewhere or achieve something it should stay that way forever. We forget that life is full of surprises and we need and want different things in different seasons of life. It is okay to change and let go and grow into new directions, and the trees help model that for us. They remind us every season that they too work so hard and put all their resources toward beautiful leaves and fruit, and then they show us how to allow them to fall away, to become nutrients for animals, people, and the earth. They don't hold on, they let go, knowing that there is beauty and gold that can only come from allowing old things to go. We never really lose anything, love is always there underneath, and gold is always inside. But sometimes we only get to see it when we let it go, give it away, and allow it to nourish someone else or nourish our own next growing season.

Nurturing compassion in yourself and in the world

Go outside today and hug a tree or just simply rest with your back against a tree. Yes, you can do it. In the song "Nature," by East Forest and Ram Dass it says, "When you hug a tree you are hugging yourself." And if you really can't, then just do something that gets your hands in the earth or your feet in the water. As you connect just allow some of nature and her wisdom to rub off on you, helping you trust that love never really leaves and supporting you in your ever-evolving nature. Getting houseplants can be a great way to be connected to nature more often.

Give a fruit of yours away today. Maybe it is an object that was special or helpful to you or perhaps it is knowledge or wisdom you have, but let it be something that feels a bit hard to let go of and truly feels like a treasure you are sharing. Allow your life to be of service to someone else.

30

Love with food

I am the worst at eating mindfully. I always have so many things I want to do that to sit down and only eat my food is challenging for me. I am often shoveling food quickly down my throat, missing out on the melody of flavors and texture and nutrients. I so rarely set the table for myself, taking the time to put down a placemat, or display a flower or candle. And sometimes I barely even consider sitting down, let alone selecting a beautiful location indoors or out to sit. But when I take the time it truly is an act of love. An act of appreciation for all the hard work and effort that went into my meal, and not just by me (as often not a lot is done by me as I still haven't taken to cooking as a creative endeavor), but from the farmers and the earth and all the steps in between.

If you are anything like me, food is a complex topic and the last thing it ever needs is another helping of shame. But it does need some kind attention because, if we skip this, we miss a huge built-in opportunity love has provided us to nourish ourselves several times a day, every day. It takes courage to slow down and to really enter into a friendship with food. Often times the critical voice and the voice of fear and outside voices can be really loud in this area. My journey with food and health and my body could be a whole other book, and maybe it will be one day, but at this moment in time, I think the most beautiful gift we can give ourselves and our world is to be aware of and connected with where our food comes from and to form a loving relationship with food. And that takes slowing down, paying attention, and not skipping the growing process.

Anytime we bring attention to something we become more invested in it, and it has the potential to then become a powerful source of healing for ourselves and the world. When we begin to become aware of the real costs to people, animals, and the earth, we usually become much more reverent and appreciative of just how much of a gift food, or any purchase, is to us. We begin to make compassionate choices, as we are able, for our body and also for the planet and her health and creatures. And when we view something as a gift, we enjoy it, we savor it, we allow it to be so much more than a carbohydrate or a protein, it becomes a relationship we can cherish and nurture. There are so many temptations around to go faster and eat more junk, and the grocery stores present us with only instant gratification through ripe or ready items, but I think love desires more than speed eating and a pitstop refuel of calories. Love wants us to know that we are being fed at a soul level. The earth offers us her fruits, her medicines. When we take the time to choose compassionate foods and then choose to slow down and truly be present with the gifts we have been given, I think it makes a world of difference.

Nurturing compassion in yourself and in the world

Invite compassion into your relationship with food today. Create an ambiance that reflects love to you and then spend time enjoying your space and your sweet nectar of a meal. For fun, if you normally use a fork, you could try eating with chopsticks, it will really slow you down. I also find eating outside helps me to slow my pace. Begin to tune in and notice how you feel and start where you can with compassionate, whole food choices and practices. Let go of labels and put down perfection.

Support those companies and farmers who are committed to slow and saying yes to letting nature do her own thing on her own timeline. Maybe you support your local co-op and farmers by getting an organic produce box or, if you consume animal products, by buying from non-factory farmed sources. Find a plant powered restaurant and patronize them, or add more plant-based meals to your diet. If you can, plant your own garden or fruit trees (or even indoor herbs) and begin developing a respectful relationship with where your food comes from.

31

Love is in every season

I used to be so out of touch with my own natural rhythms and the seasons of the planet. As I learned how to appreciate and honor my monthly cycle, thanks to Red School, it helped me to see beauty in seasons and to trust my needs at different times. I learned that we must care for ourselves, even when we seem needy or completely useless, and that those times are valuable and all a part of the whole, just as winter is necessary for springtime to occur. It is often the times when things are the hardest or most stressful, or when everything feels really dark or dead, that we just try to survive, and we forget or feel that we cannot or should not care for ourselves.

I think self-compassion is a lot like watering – we have to do it more frequently in harsh or challenging conditions. Often those are the times we do it less, thinking we aren't worthy or don't have the time or energy to add anything else. But the truth is, we won't survive, as I unfortunately learned when I took a vacation during a Texas summer and my bonsais only got watered every other day by a kind friend. We too will dry up and die, or be severely stunted and damaged, and take a long time to recover.

We also forget that growth can be stressful too, and when we are experiencing changes, even good ones, we probably need extra support. Even if we sometimes feel like a potted plant and can't control our environment, we can be in charge of how we care for and love ourselves well, nourishing ourselves fully in different conditions and seasons.

When I was in a season of applying more self-compassion due to good, but still stressors of a move and all that goes with that, I met up for lunch with a Daring Way™ colleague. I was really feeling like daily I was doing something kind for myself – the self-compassion break, taking time to apply essential oils, noticing when I needed movement or a tea break and taking it even if everything was a complete mess and very unfinished. She said she too had been practicing self-compassion and then shared with me something that I will always treasure and only wish a younger me could have done at certain times in my life. She said she had had a hard relationship stressor but had plans scheduled that she really wanted to show up for and be able to be fully present. She said she decided to follow through even though she felt like doing anything but that. She knew she had to take care of herself so she set a timer on her phone to go off every hour. When it did, she would stop and say something kind to herself. Every hour! I loved hearing about that so much. Let's treat ourselves to succulent necessary love in every season, committing to thrive and love ourselves the best that we can no matter what comes our way!

Nurturing compassion in yourself and in your world

Notice what your environment is like right now and what season your body is in. What would it look like to water and how often do you need to do it? Give yourself a really nurturing environment today.

Self-compassion leads to greater compassion. Since we can't always know what others are going through, be generous with others you encounter today whether through your finances, gifts, or presence. You might just be watering someone during a really dry season.

32

Love is always watching

Does it really matter how you do things when no one is watching? Absolutely. Love is always watching. Love is about watching how you do things and believing that if you pour love into even the smallest or mundane acts, especially the ones that no one will ever see or know about, it truly does matter and make a difference. And, in addition to love, often people are watching, even if you don't know. You know that feeling you get when you see someone just doing their job but they are doing it in a kind and thoughtful way? For me it can be as simple as happening to see how different service providers leave packages, the ones who just drop them versus the ones who take the time to carefully place. That feeling I get when I see the latter makes me want to do everything with a bit more quality and a bit more care, no matter who may or may not be watching, because it will be impacting and changing me.

There is also the magic that happens when you experience love in a place you never expected to be watching for it, such as at the post office, the DMV, or the voting polls. I was waiting in line to vote one year and a man who had just turned in his ballot stopped at another man in front of me who was just signing in. He simply put his hand on the other man's shoulder and said, "Hey friend, if no one has told you today, you are loved and appreciated," and went on his way. They obviously knew each other to some degree, but I still watched as the man who had received those unexpected words lit up, and as everyone who had witnessed it felt the change in the energy in the room. I had a tear in my eye because it was such as surprise in that environment. And it changed me. Instead of staying closed and just showing up to do my civic duty, my heart opened and as I left I held the door for two women, one who was using a walker, one who looked like she was a daughter or a friend, and both who looked like they wanted to be doing anything else and may have been a bit annoyed with each other. I told them both, "Just in case no one has told y'all today, you are both greatly loved and appreciated." The older woman lit up and smiled and the younger woman said, "Thank you, I really needed that today."

Love is always watching how you show up in your life and to see if you appreciate each moment as it is and treat this life as the sacred gift it is. We are building our lives in each moment, and we don't want to wait to pour love into our actions until it is something we deem important or we know someone is watching. We want to always be practicing living with so much love that we become love. Becoming so that we can't help but act in the most loving and present ways no matter if we are doing a household chore for the millionth time, performing a service we think no one will see, or showing up in big public ways. Love is always watching your heart in all matters.

Nurturing compassion in yourself and in the world

Set a timer and for that amount of time try to mindfully and with love perform your ordinary daily actions. Pretend love is watching and notice what it feels like to bring your full attention and heart to each task.

Acknowledge that you see people making a difference. Leave a review for a business you like, call a manager, or write a thank you note to an organization. Let people know that love is always watching.

33

Love waits

Love does wait, and for those of you who remember the abstinence campaigns in the early 90s, no that is not what this reflection is about, although I could definitely also write on how that and other messages about sex really messed me up. To illustrate what I mean by love waits, please allow me to use another normal bodily reference though – acne. Even if you have never had intense struggles with it, I think most of us know the irritation of a zit or a pimple, especially one that is huge and red and painful, and yet, it is not ready to be popped or healed. Oh, it is the worst, right?! You still try to pop it because it hurts and it is ugly and you want relief, but you literally just have to WAIT until it is ready and all the forcing you tried just made it hurt worse. And so, you go through life with this reminder on your body for all the world to see that you have dead skin cells just waiting to be expelled.

To me this is such a hard place to be, and yet we are literally going through this cycle of waiting all the time. I need to take a lesson from my new vacuum cleaner. Our family hadn't bought a new vacuum in 14 years and because it brings out my perfectionist part and exhausts my already easily decision-fatigued self, my husband had researched and picked this new one out. I was loving the new vacuum and thinking my husband had nailed it, but then was shocked to discover that after 20 minutes on its max capacity, it was done. Literally, I could not use it anymore and had to wait approximately five hours while it charged. Whoa. I mean when my laptop goes dead I can just plug it in and keep working. I literally had to leave half of the house unvacuumed, I was forced to wait. What a blessing to be given such a literal reminder about how when we have done everything we can do, it is necessary and good to do nothing and wait and recharge, even if we can see so much more that we want to change and complete.

We are constantly in cyclones of change because life is complex and chaotic, and even though we think we need instant relief, what we really need is increased compassion. We need to be gentle with ourselves and these places and seasons of waiting. It is so hard when we can literally see the new life and times ahead, or even more so when we can't and the dark unknown is surrounding us, but we still have to wait patiently for all the old to be released on its on timing. Committing to stop forcing the process along, which often doesn't help and only causes more pain, and instead applying some compassion and kindness for all that occurring, is how love waits.

Nurturing compassion in yourself and in the world

Go outside and look at the moon. The moon goes through the process of waxing and waning each month, allowing time for the new, full integration, and then release. Spend time with it when it is in the place you are in and let it reassure you about the natural rhythm of change.

Send someone a care package, a plant or flowers, or note of love. Maybe someone has moved or changed jobs, is dealing with an illness or loss, is in a stressful challenging season, or you just know that they are hard on themselves and don't love themselves well. Fill it up with comforting items that encourage and remind them to take some time to wait with love.

34

Love takes time to be

It is amazing how much of the time I am not actually present. I treat the day like one giant check-list, even in the things I enjoy doing, I am thinking about the next thing, and just getting through. I rush from task to task, and wonder why I am rushing to death. I never exit the doing mood and forget that I am a human being and neglect to be and love where I am. Learning to take my time is a continual lesson and practice for me. I have so much resistance to taking my time because my critical voice is telling me, "You will run out of time," "You will miss out on things that are for you," "You won't do enough," "You will get behind," and so on. But love keeps telling me, "There is time," and "It is okay to take your time," and I know that when I do, everything changes, and, almost always, all is revealed in time when I stop forcing my agenda and timelines.

Usually I experience just being on silent or meditative type retreats that I try to do at least once a year. The leaders of these retreats often encourage you not to fill the space with your usual intake, even if it is good things. And so, when I listen, I find myself just sitting outside in nature, no agenda, not even reading or knitting or listening to music or making art, but literally, just taking the time to be. Writing that still gives me the shivers! I hate to go anywhere without those comfort items, but so often, in addition to all the good they can be, they can also be numbing or productivity in disguise and can keep me from truly slowing down and being present in my life. It is so good for my soul when I practice being during those times, and the silence helps me exit trying to perform or think of the perfect things to say to others and become aware of my often limiting and negative inner dialogue. But when I return from those soul-tuning experiences, the doing often creeps back in, and I just do not take time to be. I find myself back to forcing my plans in the day, no matter if I hear whispers from my soul of another plan or rhythm that is in more alignment with that time.

Sabbath is a spiritual discipline where you take a day to rest, unplug, and if you do something, you do only what brings you life. It is what I have to practice regularly to keep my soul calibrated. Sabbath is about trusting that love provides for you and that it is okay to just be. And it is hard. But once I have started it is not as hard (except the desire maybe to check my messages or feeds), because wow does it refresh and refuel me. And it frees me from the lies my critical voice was telling me before I started – lies such as I can only rest when I am done or when things are perfect. Because the truth is, creating a life is never done, and there is no such thing as perfect. Love directs that we stop hustling in the fear that if we stop we won't get it all done or we won't be okay. Love directs that we rest and trust that there is more to life than our to-do lists, accomplishments, and goals. Love tells us life is about enjoying and being connected with the earth and with each other and with love. If you are fearful of stopping to rest and refuel, you may need love to guide you in the ways of Sabbath.

Nurturing compassion in yourself and in the world

Don't do things just to get done, instead mindfully savor your experiences today. If it is calling to you, maybe even try out a Sabbath practice today or this weekend. It is such a great way to honor your needs to play and rest well. You don't have to take a full day, it could just be a couple of hours, even thirty minutes will work wonders. Just commit to unplugging from technology and work and focus instead on what brings you life and rest.

Support someone else being today. Consider volunteering or donating in some way that shows how valuable each and every one of us are and maybe helps give someone permission to rest no matter what they might be going through because they know love is with them. This could be as simple as making your online purchases starting at AmazonSmile so that a percentage of what you order supports a cause you pick.

35

Love invites you in for a bowl of tea

I bought an expensive cast iron tea pot set in college. It was one of those things that I just had to have and was going to use it all the time. And you know how the story goes, I used it a bit and then it was just a decorative place to collect dust and rarely saw any tea. Working a lot from home as a new entrepreneur 10 years later, I turned back to tea as a ritual because I needed something to help my afternoon slumps when I felt dejected and that everything was a mess and I could not go on. And it was not just the stimulant or warmth of tea I needed, it was the ceremony of it. I mean, pouring water into a microwave safe cup and hitting the two-minute button and then sticking a tea bag in is much less daunting energy-wise when everything already feels too much, but something happened when I started taking the time in the afternoon to stop and slow down and ritually make tea - Pouring the water into the kettle, waiting as it heated up on the stove, gathering some loose-leaf tea into the fancy tea pot, adding the hot water, waiting as the tea brewed, and then sitting down to really enjoy.

Tea is plant medicine, and even though I was clueless as to the history and spirit of tea that had been moving people throughout history, as with anything in life, when you start to pay attention, you see there is so much more beneath the surface. Tea has since become much more than an afternoon tea break ritual, tea has become a TEAcher and she has led me on an unexpected journey. Discovering and becoming part of Global Tea Hut and receiving sustainably produced and pure tea every month along with a work of art and wise magazine has been transformative in my life way beyond taking a tea break. I laugh now to think that the expensive pot was fancy and the tea I used quality, but that is okay, because tea meets us wherever we are, and it is never about being perfect or having the right things, it was about being open to what your teacher has to give you.

Anything can be our teacher if we let it, but we have to come into relationship. And that means investing our time and energy, and engaging with reverence and great care. We can't experience or do something once and expect it to change us. We can't mistreat or skimp on a relationship and expect true love. Love is always waiting to offer us a bowl of tea - simple, large, pure leaves in a bowl with hot spring water. She is always ready to serve us and we can come and drink a bowl or two and go on our way. But if we want to grow in the way of love, we need to spend time with her, steeping silently in her waters, listening and filling up with a new wisdom.

Nurturing compassion in yourself and in the world

Try simply having tea today. It doesn't matter how you make or prepare the tea, but make sure the only thing you do is drink your tea. As my TEAcher Wu De has written, "Make tea a practice of good for nothing, doing nothing!" Use both hands to hold your tea, bringing your full attention to the moment. Savor your tea time. Look for how her warmth and patience might rub off on you long after you are done.

Serve someone tea today. There is nothing like receiving a bowl or cup of love and comfort. A motto of Global Tea Hut is, "Love is changing the world. Cup by cup, bowl by bowl." Or you could always give or send someone some tea too so they can stop and experience her as well.

36

Love gets off at your stop

I never wanted to travel to a foreign country where I couldn't speak the language by myself, but when you are following love sometimes you have to go outside your comfort zone. Thanks to the love of tea, I went to Taiwan to stay and serve at Global Tea Hut's tea center. I had many tears before I left and during, and it was definitely a stretching growth experience for me. And it was an opportunity for love to show up. Because sometimes when I live a life that I can control, do everything on my own, and am always planned and prepared and able to meet my own needs, I leave little opportunity to be amazed at the lengths love can go. It seemed my fate was to travel during holidays while I was there, and the day I was heading back to the airport hotel, was just such a day. All the money in the world couldn't buy me a seat on the train, and I had to take my two big bags and huge backpack filled with a month of tea travels, and take my chances. There was absolutely nowhere to sit, but at the front of one of the train cars there was actually space to stow my luggage, and instead of standing there staring at everyone sitting down, I just walked out and stood in the vestibule between the train cars where I could still see my bags but have some space. I breathed a sigh of relief at having things settled, and as my ride wasn't long, in two stops I knew I would be off.

At the next stop, anxiety returned, in the form of panic. I had never seen so many people get on at a stop, in fact, I am not sure how everyone was able to squeeze on. Before I knew it, the aisles in the train cars were full of people standing and the vestibule where me and another man had once been standing peacefully, was packed tighter than a sardine can. I was literally backed into the corner and couldn't move, and I may have been hyperventilating. What had been an easy couple of steps to grab my bag a moment ago, might as well now have been the red sea, and I was due off at the next stop. So, I did the only thing I knew how to do, I prayed. I prayed for a miracle, because I literally did not know what to do. Not being able to speak the language and tell people what I needed, I didn't see how if I didn't have my bags before we stopped there would be time to go against the sea and get them and get off before the train was moving again. I was cursing ever walking even a couple steps away from my bags, even though I never saw that huge wave of people coming, and I was praying without ceasing. And then, in my paralyzed praying state, it happened.

From the vestibule, I saw someone parting people and walking down the aisle in the train car, and they stopped where my bags where. I couldn't believe it... their bag was behind my two bags and it looked like they were preparing to get off too. As they pulled out my bag to get to theirs I gestured and shouted radically and made it clear in universal sign language it was mine and I was getting off next too.

109

Somehow, both my bags got to me. I had my bags. I couldn't believe it. But because we were so squashed together, I couldn't get my bags the way I needed to be able to move them as a unit so I was awkwardly holding one and wondering how on earth I would position and be able to get everything off still. I must have looked like I felt, trapped under some heavy burdens, some real, some imagined, because the next thing I knew the doors were opening and a person gestured to one of my bags and having little choice, I took a leap of faith and let them take it and lead me off the train. We managed off and they put my bag on top of the other one and then, they got back on the train. They got back on the train. I am pretty sure I was sobbing. God had parted the red sea and delivered my bags to me and then love literally went out of her way to get off at my stop and help me with my bags.

Nurturing compassion in yourself and in the world

When is the last time you were out of your element or in over your head? Maybe it is time to trust love and be willing to stretch in an area that is outside of your comfort zone. Try doing one thing that scares you today and lean on your friendship with love to help you. She loves when you need her and she loves to show off.

Help someone remember that we are all each other's brothers and sisters and that we never truly have to travel alone by praying to be love today. You may never know you are even being a miracle, or you may never know the extent of what your kindness meant, just as the person who probably hopped off to help with my bag thought it was no big deal. But know that your willingness to be a part of love was a miracle for someone today.

37

Love doesn't pick you up from the airport

I had just been on the biggest solo adventure of my life, traveling to a foreign country to learn about and serve tea for almost a month, and exhausted doesn't even begin to describe how I felt. I was finally headed home and the anticipation was building. I couldn't wait for my favorite comfort food meal – tofu cashew cheese nachos – and of course to see my husband and my little dog. After more than a decade of marriage I wasn't expecting or wanting flowers at the airport, but my mind did wonder, will he actually park and come in and get me, or will he just be in the pick-up circle as usual?

I had noticed that he hadn't read my text when my first flight landed in California (I love that you can turn on those read reminders just for certain people), but I wasn't too concerned as I knew he was probably sleeping. When I landed in Texas and turned on my phone and saw he still hadn't read my California text, my stomach dropped. I still wasn't too worried that something bad had happened as we had talked right before I left, but I just had a feeling this was not going to go well and I texted him I had landed. After we had taxied and as I was walking down the gangplank he called. His voice told me everything. He had the time down wrong and thought my flight was coming in several hours later. He had JUST woken up. He was going to leave right now. I don't remember exactly what I said, I am sure it wasn't pretty, and I hung up and just started crying.

At one point in our marriage, this event would have been a disaster. Because I wouldn't have been able to be compassionate with my messy and hurt self, there would have been no way I would have responded to him with anything but blame and anger. Years of self-compassion practice paid off, because after I hung up, I gathered my compassion and I was kind to myself and to him. Still crying, I acknowledged how much this sucked and was disappointing, mostly because I was so tired and had been looking forward to not having to figure anything else out and to just be taken care of and relax. I told myself I could get through this just like everything else and I appreciated that this wouldn't be my first rideshare experience and that I had cell service and signs in English. Then, I called my husband back and told him not to worry about getting me. I knew from his voice he was utterly exhausted from a season of beyond long working hours and taking care of everything so I could have this adventure, and neither one of our time would be well spent with the long drive it would take him just to reach me. I told him it was okay and that I loved him because I knew he was probably going to be hard on himself, even though this man has been there for me and supported and loved me in unbelievable and unconditional ways. And, because I am still a work in progress, I had to add on that he better have some damn nachos ready for me when I arrived. I realized that day love doesn't pick you up from the airport because you can't leave love behind. Your heart is always packed with a deep well of compassion you only have to dip into. It is okay to travel light because compassion is there for and with you in all of the unexpected moments and challenges of life, just don't forget about her.

Nurturing compassion in yourself and in the world

Research shows that loving touch can actually impact us quicker than our kind words can. Today try giving yourself a hug, putting a hand on your heart, or massaging your shoulders or face. Remember your body is always with you and available to comfort you.

The next time you have the opportunity, be generous in your interpretation of a situation. Don't make it personal or make up a negative story, give yourself compassion and what you need and try and see the other person's perspective. Look at it as a great chance to receive and give compassion.

38

Love for the right reasons

Intention really does matter, and it really does change things. In my perfectionism and anxiety, I used to clean my home obsessively. Everything had to be spotless. I took pride in my home always looking good, it was about the outer appearance, and about controlling my environment when I couldn't control a whole lot else. As I allowed imperfection a place in my life and my home, my cleaning escapades calmed down, and although I was still neat and clean, I had dust on my floor boards and the other normal hazards of living most people have. Then, I went and stayed at the Tea Sage Hut in Taiwan, thanks to Global Tea Hut, and I learned about cleaning in a whole new way. I learned about the intention and the energy behind cleaning, about how it honors ourselves and others and creates new space and room.

I came home and literally moved and cleaned everything in my house. I started laughing as I saw in myself again this crazed cleaning lady, but this time it was so different. I didn't try to do it in one day like I used to, unable to stop until I dropped. I took my time, and I prayed, simplified and honored, and added in beauty. It took a long time, but I finally arrived at a place where everything had been shifted and given some TLC. I could feel the difference palpably in my surroundings, and in myself. I wasn't cleaning any more to impress others or to control what I could, I was cleaning out of love, because I wanted to love my belongings well and I wanted people to feel love and respect and care when they entered my space.

I can't tell you how many times I have only loved on the surface. Often, I didn't even know I was doing it because I never stopped to see where my heart really was and just did the things I thought I should, no matter if they wore me out or caused me anxiety or were not the best use of my gifts. I would cycle between doing everything and then completely withdrawing because I did not know how to say no or care for myself. I think it is always good to be open to growing and serving where needed, but it is also good to remember we can't love long-term if we do it in a way that is damaging or not sustainable for us. Even though I know this, I keep forgetting, like at the Tea Sage Hut. There I battled with wanting to serve like everyone else was and look good, but I also knew if I didn't take that nap, or take that introvert space, I would be useless and unable to keep showing up. Just because someone else can, doesn't mean you should, even if they don't understand or perhaps even judge your limitations (which sadly sometimes I still catch myself also forgetting and doing to others). Love wants us to look on the inside and be honest about our feelings, limitations, and desires, and most importantly, to honor them and love only for the right reasons.

Nurturing compassion in yourself and in the world

Be honest with yourself today. Take an inventory and see if you are doing something or not doing something based on a should, what other people might think, worries about hurting someone's feelings, or from wanting to be viewed in a certain way. I really do not think it helps when we do things for the wrong reasons, so consider releasing those things that aren't truly coming from your heart space. Tend to yourself with love today, committing to, over time, clearing and cleaning out and making room for the things you really do love and the ways you do want to show it.

To move from roots that are deep in loving intentions and not tethered to any outcomes or expectation, try loving someone without them knowing today. Savor the reward that you put love into the world, and trust that it does indeed still make a difference for us all.

39

Love meditation

I knew about the loving kindness meditation thanks to Kristin Neff's guided meditation on her website and I learned that it was also called Metta meditation from my wise restorative yoga teacher. Metta is about sending love and well wishes towards yourself and others, including those that are hard for you to love. While you can tailor the meditation as you like, it usually consists of three or four phrases along these lines: May I/you be happy; May I/you be free from suffering/healthy; May I/you be peaceful/live with ease; May I/you be safe.

I had used the love meditation in my work with clients and at events or groups, but honestly, I didn't have much personal practice with it. That changed after I spent several weeks at Global Tea Hut's Tea Sage Hut. There they practice morning and evening meditation, and although you are welcome to practice any quiet meditation you like, they practice Zazen meditation followed by Metta meditation. I had already been practicing seated, breath-focused meditation in some form or fashion fairly consistently for several years, but usually never for more than 20-30 minutes, and I had never combined loving kindness or my prayer practice with it. After I finally found the right combination of pre-stretching and how to sit to prolong my legs falling asleep and/or hip pain as long as possible, and after I finally let go of the exhausting voices that were focused on if I looked like I was doing it right and a good meditator to others, I grew to love the hour-long twice a day sessions. I especially loved how they taught to offer loving kindness and the merits of your practice back to the world and all of life.

Now, loving kindness is synonymous to me with my breathing meditation practice, I don't do one without the other. I think love works a lot like the breath, you are breathing in love for yourself and breathing it back out to the world. It only makes sense now that the two practices would go together as just like you can't hold in your breath, you can't hold in love. And just know, that this morning, I sent love to you: May you be happy, healthy, and holy. May you be free from suffering. May you be peaceful.

Nurturing compassion in yourself and in the world

As Brené Brown tells us in her book *The Gifts of Imperfection*, "We can only love others as much as we love ourselves," so practice Metta for yourself first. Kristin Neff has a Self-Compassion Metta version on her website, *self-compassion.org*, you can download for free if you have a hard time or need guidance.

Practice Metta for someone else today. Bring their image to mind and send them love.

40

Love becomes

Ever since I took Brené Brown's e-course and got trained in her work, I have never stopped practicing and teaching her guideposts for Wholehearted Living, adding in my own touches of essential oils, yoga, and creative exercises I have developed over the years. The very first time I led the experience, we had canvases I had made for each guidepost, and then during each session we all added our own marks or words to the quote or images I had started us off with. The quote from Brené Brown I used for practicing self-compassion and letting go of perfectionism was, "When we become more loving and compassionate with ourselves and we begin to practice shame resilience, we can embrace our imperfections. It is in the process of embracing our imperfections that we find our truest gifts: courage, compassion, and connection." Under the quote I wrote "Practice Self-Compassion." I had a helper that first year, a therapist in training, and I can still remember when she added "BECOME Self-Compassion" under where I had originally written "Practice Self-Compassion." I remember thinking when I saw it, "How do you become self-compassion?"

To be honest, and sorry if this is a let-down, but I still don't fully know. But I do know that I am not the same since I first started practicing self-compassion. I have become someone who knows and trusts her compassionate voice. The critics in my head and in the world don't stop me anymore, or at least not for as long or as deep. Thanks to practicing meditation, I catch myself when I am listening to only my critical voice, and I choose instead to see myself and the world through love, over and over again. It is so much easier now to be kind to myself, to tell myself "I love you," and that I am precious. I believe more in the gentle power of compassion to move me in ways that would have never happened with the hate and venom I used to pour into my life. I could not have dared nor discovered in the ways I have and become who I am now without the support of my own love, and all those who have lit the way. Understanding my true taproot has always been in love, as it is with all beings, helped me let go of feeding fear and perfectionism. I know to get the depth I want in life, I have to inhale and exhale love deeply.

I also believe that we need each other as we continue to travel down this path of compassion and love. We each have wisdom and love that we need to give ourselves and share with others on this journey. And that means that we have to keep showing up, as imperfect and messy as we are, for ourselves and for each other. Thank you for listening to your soul and allowing yourself this experience. Please keep taking the time to listen to love and go towards the next light she is showing you, even if it seems uncertain or scary. Love has always been guiding you and will never leave you as you keep becoming all that you have planted. You continuing to create a nurturing environment in your life will truly change the world. Remember that love is a gentle teacher and always has your best interests at heart. Do everything with love and give yourself time. If you push past a stretch into pain, that is not love. Keep walking in the light you have, trust you are doing the best you can, rest, and stay open. Make lots of mistakes and learn as you go. Begin again, and again, and again. And remember, everything supports you, and you are loved.

Nurturing compassion in yourself and in the world

Spend some time today reflecting on this 40-day experience in whatever creative way works for you. Maybe you listen to the playlist again, write a letter for yourself about what you have learned, draw out some seeds that have grown for or surprised you, or journal about any shifts you have noticed.

Put some thought into what you will carry with you from this book. How do you want to continue to nurture yourself and the world? Notice what invitations or days really resonated with you and commit to continue to lean into loving yourself and all of creation deeply.

Acknowledgements

Dear critical voice,

I know I don't say it enough, so I wanted to publicly thank you today. I have misunderstood and judged you most of my life. I thought you were out to get me and always assumed that your intentions were evil. I experienced hurt and felt like I had to hustle to make you happy, but I was never perfect enough.

I realize now that is how you are made. You will never stop criticizing and pointing out concerns because that is who you are. You are a gift, and you have always been trying to help me, in your own way. I understand now that you only wanted to keep me safe, help me to fit in and be able to survive, and produce my best work. I really do appreciate that.

I also realize that you and I are not the same. You see, for a long time, I mistakenly thought your voice was the same as my own. Thanks to meditation, I have been able to see we are different and have concluded that there is nothing wrong with you, and there is nothing wrong with me.

Knowing this, I promise to no longer try to shut you out and down, and I also promise to give more voice to all the other sources of wisdom and gifts I have been given. I was never meant to listen to you alone. Your purpose is to be a part of the whole.

Thanks for all your help and please forgive me for all the ways I have judged you. It took learning to be compassionate with myself to discover I could also see you with compassionate eyes. I won't ask so much of you anymore, and I am glad you are a part of the family.

Love,
Lee Ann

"Live more mindfully, write a new chapter in your life, reclaim your wholeness and feel reverence in your heart, for by planting these seeds you will create a beautiful garden that will bear fruit to sustain your soul and nourish your spirit for eternity."

—Micheal Teal

Made in the USA
Lexington, KY
11 May 2019